To Barbara —

Happy Birthday
this 33rd!

Love,
Jean

THE
COUNTRY HOUSE
COOKERY BOOK

Christian Hesketh
Elisabeth Luard
Laura Blond

St. Martin's Press
New York

for Betty and Walker

Library of Congress Catalog Card Number 85-61904

ISBN 0-312-17038-6

First published in Great Britain by
Century Hutchinson & Co. Ltd.

First U.S. Edition

10 9 8 7 6 5 4 3 2 1

Contents

1
THE MISTRESS
OF THE HOUSEHOLD
THROUGH THE AGES

2
COUNTRY HOUSE MENUS

3
THE HOUSEHOLD OFFICES

4
SPECIAL OCCASIONS

THE COMING OF AGE OF VISCOUNT LUMLEY, 1878

page 255

INDEX OF RECIPES

page 262

ACKNOWLEDGEMENTS

page 264

Foreword and Acknowledgements

In the introduction that follows Elisabeth Luard could have confined herself to the rudiments of country house cooking. Instead, she has chosen to relate the kitchens to be found in many different kinds of country houses to an ever-changing society. In that society, historical events of all sorts from the Roman Conquest to the rise of the British Empire and the discovery of coal and gas have played their different parts in the development of the British kitchen. Over the centuries successive waves of immigrants have come to these shores, all of them bringing with them their own eating habits, many of which are reflected in today's menus.

At the same time, the number of those coming here was matched, if not surpassed, by that of Britons going abroad. Whether those who went found themselves in Crak des Chevaliers at the time of the Crusades, or sought pastures new in seventeenth century Virginia; whether they fought as mercenaries in the never-ending European wars, went on the Grand Tour, or looked for a Nabob's fortune in India as servants of the East India Company, nearly all of them brought home not only ideas but plants, flowers, and dishes, many of which are now regarded as home-grown. The introduction also records how over the centuries the values of foods have changed. One example of this is the oyster which in all recipes prior to the twentieth century was regarded as cheap fare, readily available. Salmon belonged to the same category.

In a book of this kind, in which the authors' interest is not confined exclusively to the kitchen, they have found it hard to stay within the limits they have set themselves. Any mention of gardens inevitably leads one to admire the prodigious efforts made by so many country house owners from the sixteenth century onwards to surround their new houses with a landscape worthy of its architectural centre. Their enthusiasm inspired the genius of Humphrey Repton and 'Capability' Brown, among many others, to satisfy their demands. A *Country House Cookery Book* at first sight appears far removed from the ambition of the 1st Duke of Montagu to plant an avenue of trees from Boughton House, his country seat in Northamptonshire, to his town house in London, but the expanding interests of country landowners led to changes in their kitchens as well. If there had been space to do so, the authors would also have spared a thought for the great agricultural reformers of the late eighteenth and nineteenth centuries; men like Coke of Norfolk, 'Turnip' Townsend, and the earlier 4th Earl of Bedford, who transformed the British kitchen by the changes they brought about in farming.

Last but not least, there would be neither foreword nor introduction, nor indeed would this book have been written at all, had not so many generous house owners acceded to requests which may all too often have seemed suspiciously like demands. To all of them, the authors are deeply grateful. We would also like to record the great debt we owe to those who have given so willingly of their time and knowledge to further our endeavours. Chief among them are John Cornforth, Gervase Jackson-Stops, Nicholas Luard, Robert Fermor-Hesketh, Geoffrey Johnson, Priscilla Wintringham-White, Mrs John London and Francis Russell. The Countess of Perth, Mrs de Wend Fenton, the Weller-Poley family and Lady Harod also helped us in all sorts of ways. For photographs of West Wycombe Park, Shugborough and Waddesdon Manor, we are indebted to the National Trust; for those of Deene Park and Glamis Castle to Messrs Jarrolds of Norwich, and Jeremy Marks/Woodmansterne Publications respectively, and to Lord Lambton for the game card. To John Barrow we owe a slide of the painting he did of Drayton House, and James Pipkin has allowed us to use his photographs of The Menagerie and Sledmere. Mr Basil King kindly photographed *The Cookmaid* for us at Gorhambury, Joe Rock the kitchen at Bardrochat and Jeremy Whittaker Courteen Hall. Finally, any number of cooking and typing problems have been sorted out by Diane Harris and Valerie Pettitt.

Christian Hesketh

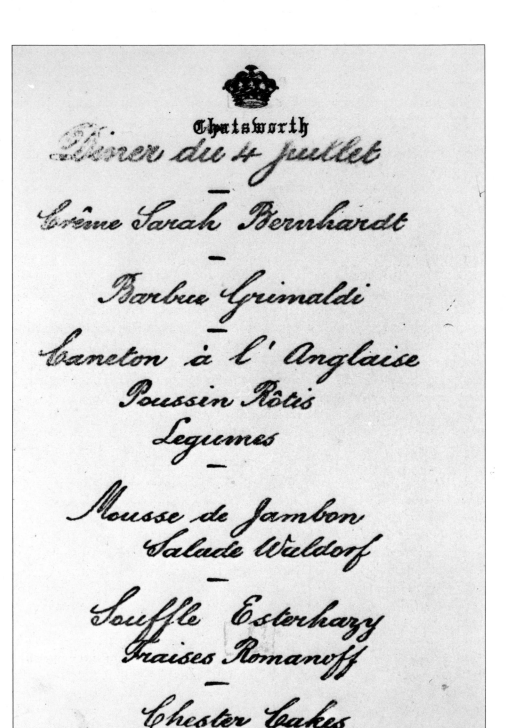

Chatsworth

Dîner du 4 juillet

–

Crème Sarah Bernhardt

–

Barbue Grimaldi

–

Caneton à l'Anglaise
Poussin Rôtis
Légumes

–

Mousse de Jambon
Salade Waldorf

–

Soufflé Esterhazy
Fraises Romanoff

–

Chester Cakes

This menu was served when King George V and Queen Mary stayed at Chatsworth on the occasion of the Royal Show on 4th July 1931. It was kindly lent by Mr James Banks who attended at the time as valet to Lord Charles Bentinck.

1
The Mistress of the Household Through the Ages

The English gentlewoman's table has a long pedigree. Give or take disruptions such as plague, pestilence and war, it has been laid for dinner for 2000 years. During the course of those twenty centuries, the lady of the manor has had to be flexible with both her favours and her menus. She has accommodated a positive Babel of guests, some of them invited and others, brandishing swords and firebrands, less welcome. Throughout, the wise gentlewoman has kept her peace and inspected the various goods they brought with them. Having chosen the ones that appealed to her, she took careful note in her household book while, at the same time, making space for the human arrivals at her table and for the stores in her commodious larders.

The modern dinner-party menus generously contributed to this book by the present owners of some of Britain's most beautiful country houses reflect her flexibility. Country house food has never been exclusively English – or indeed Scottish, Welsh or Irish. Rather it is a blend of styles and traditions acquired over the centuries from many different countries and cultures, although relying always on the excellence of the raw materials available from farmyard, garden, forest, moor and stream to dictate the composition of the feast.

In the nineteenth century, a gentlewoman's invitation might be to spend an evening in the graceful dining-room at Petworth where Turner was so frequent a guest, or amid the splendour of Chatsworth, or in the elegance of Hawksmoor's masterpiece of Easton Neston. The kitchen table would be laden with pheasant, hare and venison; from the gardens came herbs such as fennel, mint and rosemary, delicate salad leaves and tiny fresh-picked vegetables; stream and river supplied speckled trout and plump, pink-fleshed salmon; from the farm there was thick yellow cream and new-laid eggs; bowls of pot-pourri with violet and rose petals scented the hall. Add to this a French chef's skill, recipes picked up on the Italian Grand Tour, twenty years' experience in the best kitchens of the Raj, and the guests had every reason to be pleased with their dinner.

Welcome to the feast.

It began with the Romans. They arrived in AD 43, stayed until *c.* AD 410, and they liked their comforts. They built straight roads and sturdy bridges, as well as centrally heated villas with piped water supplies and excellent sanitary arrangements. Roman eating habits were sophisticated, and the local produce at the time was woefully inadequate to satisfy them. In compensation the invaders planted cherries, mulberries, peaches, pears, figs, damsons, quinces, walnuts, sweet chestnuts, and vines for the press. The grapes did not ripen well in the pale British sunshine, but Roman vintners knew how to make their wine palatable by mixing in a heavy sweet reduction of nectar from their Italian vineyards. They then introduced fallow deer, domestic geese, poultry, pheasants and rabbits. When the Romans eventually returned home, most of their technological innovations vanished with them. But they left behind, in addition to a network of roads, thirty walled towns and an expanded larder, numerous orchards – including avenues of cherry trees that had sprouted from cherry stones spat out by legions on the march – well-established populations of pheasant and deer, and a few vineyards.

The Saxons, who began to arrive in strength from about AD 445, settled down and built, as was their habit, communal wooden homesteads, the true precursors of the English manor house. They preferred to congregate in a tapestry-hung central hall with a cooking fire blazing in the middle. The doors of the hall were never closed and travellers were welcome to the communal board. The hall's furnishings were simple: benches surrounded a long, cloth-covered trestle table angled against a top table, reserved for the head of the house and his wife whose task was to dispense the bread. The table was piled with great joints of meat, cheese, honey, mead and ale. The brewers were women – the ale-wives – who would move among the diners, refilling their drinking horns. For entertainment and news, there were wandering gleemen who sang ballads to the accompaniment of the harp. At special feasts, the wassail, or 'loving cup', was passed around, as it still is at City of London banquets today. At weddings there would be a wedding cake – a bridal loaf baked by the bride to prove her expertise as a housekeeper. The early lady of the manor added the novelty of bagpipes and beer to her experience.

The comforts of home and the arrival, during the sixth and seventh centuries, of the Christian missionary monks – particularly the Benedictines who were farmers, fishermen, gardeners and doctors – had a calming influence on the warrior Saxons. By the time the marauding Vikings discovered the riches available along the coasts of Britain, the Saxon swords had long since been beaten into ploughshares. The pagan Danes sacked and burned the recently built churches, raped the women and pillaged the halls, before finally settling down with their newly acquired wealth to enjoy the very home pleasures they had been so busy destroying. The lady of the manor had new guests at her feast. She also acquired a Christian name, the game of backgammon, garters and several cathedrals, and she suffered the first recorded outbreak of smallpox.

The year 1066 brought the lady fresh company. Under Duke William, the Viking Northmen, having established themselves in northern France, invaded the land of their cousins in Britain. After its famous victory at Hastings, the foreign army took over the country's land and wealth from the Saxon freemen. For the conquered natives, life was suddenly changed. The new king believed in order and discipline. The lady of the manor had her land, her livestock and even her fishponds meticulously recorded in the *Domesday Book*. Her hall became a fortified Norman castle run on strictly feudal lines, and her day was divided with military precision. Duke William's instructions to his subjects were precise:

Lever à cinque, diner à neuf,	Rise at five, dine at nine,
Souper à cinque, coucher à neuf,	Sup at five, retire at nine,
Faire vivre d'ans nonante et neuf.	And you will live until ninety-nine.

For the first time since the Romans, the gentlewoman had a kitchen. Admittedly it was only a lean-to addition to the thick stone walls of the castle keep, but it was none the less a separate office for the preparation of food. Duke William himself brought over his entire French kitchen staff, and his banquets featured boar's head garlanded with flowers, peacock, crane and porpoise, all washed down with spiced wine.

The lady of the castle stocked her padlocked spice box with cinnamon, cloves and pepper bought from Continental travelling merchants. She became particularly fond of those spices whose taste and scent were strong enough to mask tainted meat. The native names of her domestic livestock were translated into French when the meat reached her table: 'sheep' became 'mutton', 'ox' became 'beef', 'calf' turned into 'veal'. Her castle keep had a cellar beneath for storage, and perhaps even a second chamber for receiving visitors during the day and for her family and favourites to sleep in at night. For diversion she had the suitably military game of chess.

Two centuries of relative peace amid the plenty of the English countryside worked its usual magic on the new arrivals. By the thirteenth century, the Norman baron no longer felt obliged to barricade his castle. He built his lady a manor house with a living-room not unlike her old Saxon hall. The hall was not as thick with smoke as it had been earlier as the fireplace was moved to the side of the room, instead of burning at its centre, and was equipped with a primitive chimney-canopy. The lady might even have a bed-chamber and glass in a few of her windows. Her new kitchen was a solid wooden structure built next to the hall for convenience in serving food at the great manorial feasts. Banquets, accompanied by minstrels, were the principal entertainment. They could not start until the priest had blessed the table, and a loaf of bread had been distributed to the beggars at the gate. The lady of the manor now had, as well as her cellar and kitchen, a meat larder, a buttery or 'butler's' (bottler's) store, and a pantry for bread, butter and cheese.

By now the household dined a little later. Dinner (the meal where meat predominates, as later housekeepers, confused by lunch and supper, defined it) was taken after the hunt at ten in the morning. The gentlewoman took to decorating her table with her realizable assets. Articles of gold and silver comprised medieval money, and the salt-cellar, the most important piece, marked a social boundary at the table's centre. The floor was strewn with rushes and herbs. Eating 'plates' were trenchers of two-day-old bread. Each man brought his own knife to carve his own and his lady's meat. The cooking of the period was, in part, a reflection of the lack of forks and plates. Guests speared huge pieces of roast meat to put on their trenchers, which they then soaked in gravy and devoured with their fingers. The left-over, gravy-soaked bread was given to the servants and the poor after the meal. Adventurous cooks made paste 'coffins' to protect the delicate flesh of domesticated fowls or feathered game from the fierce heat of the fire, and these later evolved into the modern pie. As yet the lady had no kitchen garden, and vegetables were rare and expensive. The cook had frequent recourse to the spice chest, and began to use sugar instead of honey as a sweetening agent.

The poor at the manor gate lived uncomfortable lives in turf- or thatch-roofed hovels. However, in years of good harvest, their diet of black bread supplemented by eggs and wild food and herbs may well have been considerably healthier than the rich meat-without-vegetables fare consumed at the hall. Rent was paid in work, each village was largely self-sufficient and there was little opportunity for commerce. In the growing towns, often centred round monasteries, a new merchant class, potentially land-owning and manor-building, was becoming increasingly prosperous.

At the hall the lady stoked her fires with coal as well as wood, fixed shutters on her new glass windows, played the fashionable game of bowls, and stocked her wardrobe with a satin skirt or two. Her interest in her wardrobe grew. Inspired by imports from the East, her dress became more and more extravagant. The assets of the household were transferred from the dinner-table to her sleeves, her shoes grew points, her head-dresses sprouted turrets, her jewels and brocades were ever more sumptuous. She displayed her finery at fashionable tournaments. At dinner she was entertained by jesters and jugglers. The manners of the guests at her table improved and she no longer expected guests to cut their own meat from the joint: she employed instead a gentleman carver skilled in the ritual dismemberment of the various meats. Meanwhile she equipped her much more comfortable dwelling with carpets, blankets, featherbeds and proper chimneys. For her personal convenience, she made use of various new inventions, including pins and spectacles. His lordship, in turn, acquired gunpowder and a watch.

In the middle of the fourteenth century, the noise of the feast and the laughter of the jesters died away. The Black Death, having already accounted for five million Chinese, crept across Asia into Africa and finally Europe. The terrible pestilence killed half the population of Britain in thirteen national epidemics over a period of one hundred years. Life ground to a halt. Nothing was sown or reaped. Livestock wandered untended. By the time the earth had settled on the graves, the social order had changed for ever. The lord of the manor's workforce was cut in half. Depopulation gave a market value to labour, and for the first time, the poor had something to sell. The beggar at the gate had a new cry: 'When Adam delved and Eve span – who was then the gentleman?' Within the manor house, the gentlewoman who had managed to survive the pestilence found a new amusement for her leisure: a pack of cards. If she was very fortunate, she also had a glimpse of the first manuscript cookbook, which appeared towards the end of the century.

The fifteenth century proved no kinder than the previous one. The English aristocracy tore itself apart during the Wars of the Roses over the rival royal claims of Lancaster and York. The combined effects of plague and civil war so weakened the old order that the feudal manorial system never recovered. Tenant farmers, their energies not diverted by the quarrels of the nobles, paid wages, worked the land and became a powerful new force in the countryside. In the towns, the middle classes and the merchants went on quietly building their fortunes. New and more elegant country and town houses appeared, this time with parlours and reception rooms to avoid the need to receive guests in the bedroom. From her manor house, the lady watched with interest, and adapted. There were coal fires, chimneys and cushions in the new parlours, and glazed recessed windows with comfortable benches beneath them. Candelabra hung from the beams, and carpets were warm underfoot. People began to take their meals in these snug chambers, table manners improved, appetites grew more fastidious and a few forks appeared – although only for eating fruit or 'soppys'. Those who could afford it continued to live off a narrow and unhealthy diet of huge quantities of meat accompanied by little else, and their life expectancy was correspondingly short. Meanwhile the merchant classes gained the social confidence to create gardens and courtyards for their houses, as the kings and great nobles had done before them.

The sixteenth century manor's livestock was likely to include oxen, cows, sheep, pigs and poultry. The manorial servants ate bread – less coarse than that of the peasants, not as fine as the lord's – a great deal of meat (brawn and mutton were much appreciated) as well as cheese, salt fish, pease-pottage and, to drink, home-brewed ale or cider. Manor house tables were heavy with beef, pork, mutton, game and venison, and such fish as carp, eel, pike and lampreys. Bread still served as trencher plates. White, red and sweet wines were imported, and supplemented by home-brewed ale, beer and cider. Salads (copied from middle-class tables where the mistress still remembered her more humble diet) sometimes appeared at the manorial board dressed with oil and spices. Initially regarded with some suspicion, they gradually became an established feature of the menu. Cabbages, lettuces, spinach and beetroots are mentioned in the fifteenth-century manuscript of Gilbert Kymer as being boiled with meat. The household book of Middleton Hall gives a shopping list for 1587 which includes eggs, butter, saltfish, pickled and red herrings, cheese, beef, bacon, mutton, capons, hens, ducks, plovers, beer, vinegar, sugar, pepper, prunes, and currants and raisins imported from Spain and the Levant.

The dinner hour was later: Henry VII dined at 11 a.m. In the manor, the mistress made further improvements to her kitchen offices. She now had a scullery that adjoined the kitchen fireplace, and a separate bakehouse and brewery. The larder and pantry were amalgamated. There were wine and beer cellars after the introduction of glass bottles, and the buttery disappeared and was replaced by a butler's pantry. The lady of the house now slept in a fourposter bed, had candles made of wax rather than wicks dipped in fat, ate breakfast to compensate for the later dinner hour, and took butter (formerly only used medicinally or eaten by the poor) with her bread.

England prospered under Henry VIII, who ascended the throne in 1509. The hall's young mistress was encouraged to be a Renaissance woman: lettered, learned and beautiful. She was also expected to entertain the peripatetic court lavishly at huge banquets. The entertainment was centred upon extravagant masques and pageants, precursors of Elizabethan theatre-drama. Travellers were fed and housed as they had been in Saxon times. The beggar at the gate, on the other hand, was held to be a sinner and severely punished. It was against the law to give alms as a private person, and collectors were appointed in each parish to take regular contributions from those listed as well-off to give to those listed as needy. There was a new problem to be faced by the mistress who was, as head cook–housekeeper, responsible for the health of the household and the nursing of the sick. The shadow of the plague hung heavy over the land and there were frequent outbreaks. Its origins were unknown and doctors were at their most ignorant; it was vaguely believed that the disease was carried by bad odours – particularly that of rotting fish.

At court, Henry's ambition and need for a son and heir led him into conflict with Rome. In 1534 he declared the Church of England reformed and himself its temporal head. One unfortunate if minor result of the subsequent dissolution of the monasteries was the loss of their vineyards – with a wine-producing tradition dating back to Roman times. The gentleman's cellar stocked ale, cider, metheglin and mead (both fermented honey drinks), and wine that now had to be imported, mainly from France and the Rhine, although some sweet wines such as malmsey came from as far as Crete. He might even lay in some Dutch beer, which was flavoured with hops and lasted a good deal longer than English ale. In good years, the villagers brewed their own ale from grain – barley, wheat or oats.

The mistress of the manor still used spices with a generous hand to mask and improve the salted and dried meat of winter, and salted her own butter for cooking. Her villagers were allowed to use the manorial oven to bake their bread, which could be white, brown or black. Her garden was growing too: innovations included cabbages, rhubarb, carrots, lettuces, cultivated strawberries, apricots, lemons, pippins and artichokes. For diversion there was the new craft of knitting, and steel needles for the sewing basket. For entertainment there were newly arrived fireworks and, rather more sinisterly, their close cousin the firearm.

Henry's daughter, Elizabeth I, started her long reign in 1558. It was a glorious era, the time of 'Merrie England' when the Queen's young buccaneers were sailing to the New World. They returned to present the lady of the manor with an assortment of outlandish new foodstuffs – potatoes, tomatoes, avocados, turkeys, Mexican drinking chocolate, and an odd new habit: tobacco smoking. All this came in addition to the gold, silver and gems that filled her coffers as the spoils of piracy. In response to the country's vigour and prosperity, the commercial centre of Europe began to shift towards London. England began to manufacture pins and needles, paper and fans, and many other luxuries. The woollen industry continued to grow in East Anglia. The middle classes became richer.

Some ladies of the manor changed their habits and way of life to match their new wealth. Their houses turned into miniature palaces. Everything was decorated and elaborated with painting, carving, embroidery and sculpture. In order for the finery to be better appreciated, Tudor oriel windows were installed, a novelty that did not meet with universal approval. Francis Bacon, for one, complained: 'You shall have sometimes fair houses so full of glass that one cannot tell where to be out of the sun or cold.' Bedrooms were furnished with magnificent four-poster beds and there were rich embroidered hangings everywhere. The hall, no longer the main living area that it had been in feudal days, now acted as an anteroom to the rest of the house, and the grand staircase led from it to the upper floors. The household offices contained a few additions: the architects' plans for the Elizabethan Hengrave Hall list kitchen, pantry, dry and wet larders, pastry-room, scouring-house, still-house, 'my lady's storehouse', laundry and linen-room, wine cellar and outer cellar. Also dairy, cheeseroom, outer dairy, brewhouse, bakehouse, malthouse, hophouse, hop-yard, slaughter-house, fish-house and fish-yard.

The mistress of the household now had a flower garden, an orchard and a vegetable garden, and used both flowers and sweet herbs to scent her splendid rooms. This was just as well since she still had no soap – clothes had to be washed with cow-dung (containing ammonia), hemlock and nettles, and consequently often smelled unpleasant, even to her hardy contemporary nose. When the Virgin Queen died, she left a wardrobe of 3000 dresses, so she at least was able to change her garments frequently.

As for entertainment, post-Reformation England made merry on the religious festivals such as Christmas, and christenings, childbirth and even funerals were regarded as good reasons for a party. Dancing and card-games were the fashionable indoor pastimes, while the brand-new pleasure of theatre-going was equally popular, with Shakespeare and Marlowe as its rising stars. New country pleasures included fox-hunting and travel by coach. The gentlewoman could now pull on a pair of silk stockings, and admire carnations and Dutch tulips, as well as eating the celery and cauliflower which grows in her garden.

Picnic During Hunt, Sixteenth century from *Turbervilles's Boke of Huntynge*.

James VI of Scotland accepted the throne of England on the death of Elizabeth in 1603. In the manor house the family still rose with the sun and breakfasted on herrings, salt fish, mutton chops and a bowl of *manchet*, a hot bread-and-milk porridge made with eggs, all washed down with a pint of wine and a pint of beer. The men then rode off to hunt deer or run their estates while the mistress and her daughters attended to household affairs. The huntsmen returned at noon for a large dinner, which was accompanied by more home-brewed ale and imported wine. After-dinner entertainment was likely to be cards and dancing.

The manorial household was self-contained in terms of necessities. The dairy produced milk, butter and a newly discovered delight – cream for the strawberries. There was bread to be baked, flax and wool to be spun for cloth, as well as all the business of preserving, conserving, salting, potting, candying, distilling and cooking – methods of preserving food were subjects of intense interest in the kitchen. Many women still died in childbirth, and the rate of infant mortality was so high that the survival of one child in two was a triumph. The aristocracy arranged its children's marriages, largely to augment the family income. While some family libraries were of outstanding interest, others contained no more than four or five volumes. The mistress of the house now had forks for the whole household, and used wallpaper on her walls. The village green saw its first game of cricket.

In 1620, the Pilgrim Fathers left Plymouth for North America in the *Mayflower*, and ten years later, 1000 others – women, children and men of education and fortune in their own country – made the hazardous trip across the Atlantic to the new lands of Massachusetts to establish themselves and their right of freedom of worship. They took their way of life with them, and rebuilt their manor houses, gardens, orchards and wheat fields in the colony of New England.

In England, society was polarizing. The court, as viewed by Thomas Muffet, had not curbed its appetites in the face of Puritan disapproval: 'The Spaniard eats, the German drinks and the English exceed in both.' The Puritans encouraged simplicity in behaviour and dress in contrast to the court, where the greatest art collector ever to sit on the English throne presided over Inigo Jones' masques and the frivolities of an extravagant age. By the time of the Parliament of 1642, the Roundheads were powerful enough to have many of the Cavaliers' favourite pastimes banned: theatres were closed and bearbaiting, cockfighting, horseracing and all Sunday activities apart from church-going were proscribed. The country finally erupted in a bitter civil war that divided not only the nation but also individual families. The first news-sheets appeared to keep the population abreast of events. After three years of fighting, Charles I was finally defeated at Naseby, and his subsequent trial and beheading made room for the Commonwealth. Queen Elizabeth's Merrie England was replaced by Cromwell's non-conformist Puritanism.

The mistress of the manor had to mend her manners. Her table reflected the new sobriety, and drunkenness was heavily fined. A cookery book purporting to be that of Elizabeth 'commonly called Joan' Cromwell, wife of the Lord Protector, was published after the Restoration of the monarchy. It was intended to be an instrument of propaganda, to expose the meanness and poverty of Puritan habits, although to today's eye the recipes seem extravagant and sumptuous enough for any Royalist table. Cromwell and his lady dined between noon and 1 p.m. Breakfast was taken at 6 a.m. and offered a choice of cold meats, cheese or fish, washed down with ale or beer. New culinary pleasures included the baking of biscuits. The first few pounds of tea were brought back from China. There was some confusion initially over the preparation of the new herb, and it was not unknown for innocent country ladies to drain off the water and sup the stewed leaves dressed with a little butter.

In the country mansions, life, although more sober, was comfortable enough. For example, in one week in 1654, Woburn purchased for the household: one bullock, two sheep, a calf, a quarter of mutton, a side of veal, 10 stone (140 lb) of pork, 1 pig, 2 calves' heads, 4 capons, 12 pigeons, 20 lb of butter, eggs, crayfish and a peck and a half of apples, not to mention vast quantities of bread and flour. The storeroom was well-stocked with relatively cheap spices and sugar, the products of increased trade with the East. The mistress of the house busied herself feeding the new English appetite for sweet pies, tarts and puddings. The butler's pantry now boasted a few bottles of spirits – perhaps aquavite and Irish usquebaugh. Everything was strictly organized including the kitchen offices, now neatly housed in a semi-basement or a separate wing.

The Restoration in 1660 of the 'merry monarch', Charles II, swung the social pendulum away from the Puritan ethic. Cakes and ale were back in fashion. Theatres were reopened and the Restoration comedy played to delighted audiences decked in periwigs, paint, patches and high-heeled shoes. All the previous pleasures and pastimes were re-introduced, and a great many more besides. In particular, there was a revived zest for gambling, and the game of billiards made its first appearance.

The chief chronicler of the time was the diarist Samuel Pepys, who recorded his New Year's breakfast in 1661, when his guests were treated to 'a barrel of oysters, a dish of neat's tongues and a dish of anchovies, wine of all sorts and Northdowne ale'. Restoration dinners were no less enormous, for evidence of which we have Pepys again (Mrs Pepys appears to have been chief cook): 'We had a fricasee of rabbits, and chickens, a leg of mutton boiled, three carps in a dish, a great dish of a side of lamb, a dish of roasted pigeons, a dish of four lobsters, three tarts, a lamprey pie, a most rare pie, a dish of anchovies, good wine of several sorts, and all things mighty noble, and to my great comfort.'

The feasting and merry-making stopped abruptly during the sweltering summer of 1665. On the doors of rich and poor alike appeared the legend 'LORD HAVE MERCY ON US' beneath the terrible red cross that signalled the presence of the last and most deadly plague. The death toll rose as the disease spread, fuelled by bad sanitation, the absence of any arrangements for the collection of rubbish (on which the rats that carried the plague-ridden fleas fed), and by doctors who were largely ignorant, superstitious and corrupt. Out of the capital's population of nearly half a million, 100,000 Londoners died – a tragedy that was immediately followed by the most dramatic slum clearance in British history, the Great Fire of London.

Faced with the terrible threat to her household, the mistress of the manor frantically searched her cookery books for recipes for elaborate poultices and witches brews, including such unusual and difficult-to-procure ingredients as 'moss from a murderer's skull'. Other remedies were, according to taste, rather more pleasant: students at

DINNER AT THE PEPYS'

'So my poor wife rose by five o'clock in the morning, before day, and went to market and bought fowls and many other things for dinner, with which I was highly pleased, and the chine of beef was down also before six o'clock. Things being put in order, and the cook come, I went to the office, where we sat till noon and then broke up, and I came home, whither by and by comes Dr Clarke and his lady, his sister, and a she-cozen, a Mr Pierce and his wife, which was all my guests. I had for them after oysters, at first course, a hash of rabbits, a lamb and a rare chine of beef. Next a great dish of roasted fowl, cost about 30s., and a tart, and then fruit and cheese. My dinner was noble and enough. I had my house mighty clean and neat, my room below with a good fire in it; my dining-room above, and my chamber being made a withdrawing chamber, and my wife's a good fire also. I find my new table very proper, and will hold nine or ten people well, but eight with great room. After dinner, the women to cards in my wife's chamber. The Doctor and Mr Pierce to mine, because the dining-room smokes unless I keep a good charcoal fire, which I was not then provide with. At night to supper, had a good sack posset and cold meat, and sent my guests away about ten o'clock at night, both them and myself highly pleased with our management of the day.'

From the Diaries of Samuel Pepys. 13th Jan. 1662

Eton were ordered to smoke a pipeful of tobacco every morning as a preventive measure.

During the course of the seventeenth century, there were various changes in the manor house kitchen. From the spit rose the scent of roasting chicken – poultry, previously considered meat only for the poor, was now appreciated as a delicacy by the rich. There were changes too in the order that the dishes were presented at table. The Tudor kitchen had served fish after meat, but this was now changed to the modern convention of soup, fish and then meat. The dessert was likely to be cheese, with perhaps fruit at the tables of the wealthy. The mistress's new-found refreshment of tea, coffee or chocolate encouraged her to entertain guests of her own. She was gradually becoming less of a housewife and more of a lady of leisure. A light breakfast, taken at the later hour of nine or ten in the morning and sometimes with company, pushed the dinner hour further back. New pleasures included brandy (now in bottles with cork stoppers), toothbrushes and violins – with an eartrumpet for the hard-of-hearing to catch the music.

James II's Protestant daughter Mary arrived in 1689 with her Dutch husband, William of Orange, to replace her father. Smog from coal fires was becoming a serious problem in London and William's health could not stand the damp and fog of Westminster. The king and queen took up residence at the Tudor palace of Hampton Court. The house itself was thoroughly renovated, and William laid out splendid new formal gardens in the style of Versailles. The rest of the nobility followed suit, and formal gardens were created for almost every grand household. The fashionable lady of the manor immediately had her box-hedges clipped into complicated labyrinths, and she dug up her flowerbeds and planted regiments of Dutch tulips. In her drawing-room she took her cue from the new queen and installed a tea-urn and small china tea-cups. She followed the royal example, too, in taking to travel for her health. Watering-places and spas, in particular Bath, became fashionable.

Out in the marketplace, fuelled by the productivity of the new age of machinery, the British were becoming an immensely wealthy nation. Across the Channel, the French were short-sighted enough to revoke the Edict of Nantes, which guaranteed the Huguenots religious freedom, with the result that France's hardworking population of Protestants flocked to Britain, bringing their manufacturing skills with them. The prosperous middle classes began to build increasingly grand houses of their own.

The mistress in her manor was not slow to recognize the potential in the new social equation. Shrewdly she paired off her daughters with the rich young merchants. Carefully she matched the heir to the estate with a well-dowered young banking heiress. Country mansions prospered. Sons were despatched to complete their education with the Grand Tour of Europe, and naturally they brought home foreign tastes and new recipes along with their purchases. The influx of money financed the employment of armies of servants, to whom the lady of the manor – whether merchant princess or earl's daughter – increasingly delegated her former household duties. The gentlewoman was no longer expected to spin and sew, to keep the stillroom and the dairy. Instead she knew how to dance and sing part-songs, to paint on glass and play the spinet, although in the kitchen, she did learn to make sauces and sweetmeats. She took dinner at the fashionably late hour of 2 p.m., read the first daily newspaper, and, when drawing a flower or landscape, rubbed out her mistakes with India rubber.

It was a land of peace and prosperity that Mary's comfortably middle-aged sister Anne inherited at William's death in 1702. Good Queen Anne had had seventeen children of whom not one survived beyond the age of eleven. Her habits were placid and her ample girth bore witness to a large appetite. Her meals were enormous and eating dominated her life. She could eat a whole chicken at a sitting and constantly sipped at a bowl of thick chocolate.

In her mansion, the gentlewoman, as usual, loyally followed the royal lead. A contemporary French traveller, M. Misson, reported on the English at table:

The English eat a great deal. Their supper is moderate: gluttons at noon and abstinent at night. I always heard they were great flesh-eaters and I found it true . . . The English tables are not delicately served: the middling sort of people have ten or twelve sorts of common Meats, which infallibly take their Turns at their Tables, and two dishes are their dinners; a pudding, for instance, and a piece of Boil'd Beef, and then they salt it some days beforehand and besiege it with five or six heaps of Cabbage, Carrots, Turnips or some other Herbs or Roots, well-peppered and salted and swimming in Butter: A leg of roast or boil'd mutton, dished up with the same dainties, Fowls, Pigs, Ox Tripes and Tongues, Rabbits, Pigeons, all well moisten'd with Butter. Two of these dishes, always served up one after the other, made the usual Dinner of a Substantial Gentleman or wealthy Citizen.

GEORGE IV
A voluptuary under the horrors of digestion by James Gilray (1757–1815), Victoria and Albert Museum.

Misson thought more highly of the English pudding, however, which he described as made of 'flour, milk, eggs, butter, sugar, suet, marrow, raisins etc. They bake them in an oven, they boil them with meat, they make them fifty different ways. *Blessed be he that invented Pudding.* Ah, what an excellent thing is an English Pudding!'

The gentleman of the household was not to be outdone by his lady. He became a member of a men-only dining club such as the Beef Steak, the Kit-Kat frequented by the Whigs or, the most exclusive and difficult of admission of all, the two-doored Fat Men's Club, whose members qualified for acceptance only if they stuck in the second, smaller doorway. Gentlemen found three further pleasures available to them: they could take snuff, smoke cigars and read about people very much like themselves in the first issues of the *Spectator*.

Elderly German George, Elector of Hanover, succeeded his childless cousin Ann in 1714. He left his wife behind in Germany, never learned more than a few words of English and gave up the government to a Cabinet, but he did have one enthusiasm in common with his new subjects – the bottle. The populace approved the king's habits and turned to the new cheap drink of gin. Contemporary shopkeepers' advertisements left no doubt about the qualities of the new beverage: 'Drunk for a penny, dead drunk for twopence, free straw to sleep it off.'

Meanwhile in the country mansion, the master of the house discovered port, and was increasingly obliged to stay at home to enjoy it. Smuggling and wrecking were common on the coast, and highwaymen plagued travellers on the roads. The gallows were busy and public executions common. A bowl of strongly spiced brandy punch was the order for celebrations. The squire's lady acquired new mahogany furniture to replace her Tudor oak – a wood now very scarce since most of it was in demand for building the wooden walls of the Royal Navy. Carpets and curtains were still a rarity in all but the grander mansions.

M. Misson volunteers further information on the English gentlewoman's housekeeping and habits:

> An Englishman's table is remarkably clean. The linen is very white, the plate shines brightly, and knives and forks are changed surprisingly often, that is to say, every time a plate is removed. When every one has done eating, the table is cleared, the cloth even being removed, and a bottle of wine, with a glass for each guest, is placed upon the table. The King's health is first drunk, then that of the Prince of Wales, and finally that of all the Royal Family. After these toasts, the women rise and leave the room, the men paying them no attention or asking them to stay; the men remain together for a longer or lesser time. This custom surprises foreigners, especially Frenchmen, who are infinitely more polite with regard to women than are Englishmen; but it is the custom, and one must submit.

Port and Madeira would then be put on the table. The evening ended in dancing –

perhaps a hornpipe, cotillon, reel, country dances and the minuet. Each lady drew her partner, with whom she danced all evening, by placing her fan on the table for selection by a gentleman. Dinner, particularly in London, was taken later than ever. The essayist and dramatist Sir Richard Steele noted in 1729 that the dinner hour had crept back to 3 p.m., and Alexander Pope's friend, the fashionable Lady Suffolk, dined as late as 4 p.m. In the conservative universities, the meal was still announced at 10 a.m.

Perhaps inevitably, after such an indulgent age, the latter part of the eighteenth century saw a Puritan religious revival, this time inspired by John Wesley and his Methodists. In the towns, the Industrial Revolution, fuelled by improved transport and a flourishing trade in goods such as cotton, muslin and calico from India, was building a new prosperity for many and fortunes for a few. Although George III had decreed that no tradesman could be elevated to the peerage, their sons and daughters continued to marry into the aristocracy, and the middle classes wielded increasing power through the House of Commons. Across the Channel, where most changes in fashionable life originated, French society was moving towards violent internal conflict. Contemporary opinion on the changes in British life was divided. The great Dr Samuel Johnson, fond as he was of the good things of life, had some sharp words to say on the banning of gambling at court and the new moderation in drinking and eating. Horace Walpole, Gothic novelist and letter-writer extraordinary, dated what he considered to be the beginning of the decadence of his countrymen from the introduction of tea and sugar.

The country gentlewoman rose at seven or eight to see to such light household chores as picking flowers, supervising the garden and interviewing the housekeeper to discuss the tasks of the day and the menus. She would then read or write letters until it was time to breakfast at ten. This meal lasted at least an hour and had evolved into a social occasion with plenty of conversation, sometimes involving guests or unexpected callers. The food itself was light: cakes and chocolate, very weak coffee, tea, bread and butter – the latter delicious and 'thin as poppy leaves', recorded the peripatetic Swiss Pastor C. P. Mirtz.

Dinner, as always, divided the day and was taken some time between 3 and 5 p.m. The fashionable mistress of the manor wore a house gown and left her hair undressed until after the meal. A guest invited to dinner could expect to remain in the house as late as midnight, and join his hostess for tea and supper as well. There was still no formal table placement and no entering the dining-room on a gentleman's arm. Ladies would withdraw when the tablecloth was removed for dessert and port, when gentlemen had both the leisure and the well-known English capacity for wine-drinking. The ladies, and those gentlemen who wished to retire with them, took coffee in the 'withdrawing-room'. The tea-urn and cake could be expected to arrive between six and seven. Supper was a cold buffet, with a few hot dishes if the company warranted it, and appeared between 10 and 11 p.m.

1st Course

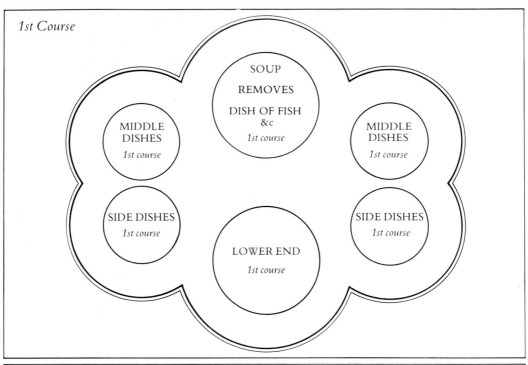

SOUP

REMOVES

DISH OF FISH
&c
1st course

MIDDLE
DISHES
1st course

MIDDLE
DISHES
1st course

SIDE DISHES
1st course

SIDE DISHES
1st course

LOWER END
1st course

2nd Course

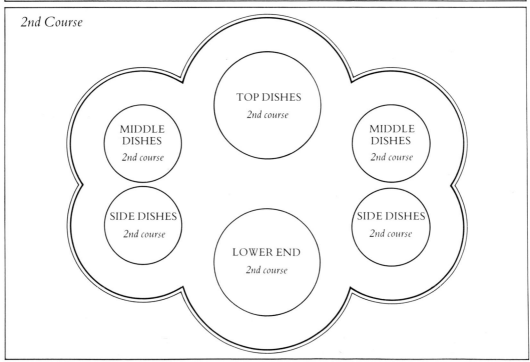

TOP DISHES
2nd course

MIDDLE
DISHES
2nd course

MIDDLE
DISHES
2nd course

SIDE DISHES
2nd course

SIDE DISHES
2nd course

LOWER END
2nd course

BEAUFRONT CASTLE

NB: Copied exactly from 1st Duchess of N's handwriting
with her spelling and capital letters etc. About 1770.

1. Soups

Herb Soup
Soup a la Reine
Birds Nest Soop
Hodge Podge
Soup Maigre (Lent ?)
Soup a la Jambe du Bois
Rice Soup
Vermacelli Soop

2. Removes

Boeuf Tremblant
Boil'd Tongue & Udder
Scarlet beef
Salmon broil'd with Shrimp &
Anchovy Sauce
Boil'd Pickled Pork & Greens
Calves head boild & broil'd
Turbot with lobster Sauce
Turkey boild with Oysters

3. Middle Dishes 1st Course

Batter pudding
Pain de Veau
Venison pastry
Marrow bones
Beans & Bacon
Pate de Godiveau
Goose Pye
Salmon Pye
Sewet Pudding
Pistachio Pudding

4. Lower End Dishes First Course

Fillet of Beef a l'italienne
Loyn of veal a la Creme
Kid
A Powder'd Goose Ro
Leg Mutton Sauce au Chevreuil
Leg of Mutton farc'd with Oysters
Haunch of Venison
Ro Pig

5. Side Dishes 1 Course

Bacon & Eggs
Fillet of Mutton Glacee
Teals with Olives
Olives of beef
Eels en Granadin
Fricasee of Rabbets
Rice flower Pudding
Laitue farci
Chickens a la Tartare
Beans & Bacon
Sho Lamb en Epigramme
Scotch Collops
Stew'd Duck with Turnips
Umble Pye

6. Top Dishes 2nd Course

Ro Larks
Pea Hen
Quails
Easterlings
Ro Bustard
Ro Turkey with
Water Cresses
Green Goose
Woodcocks
Pheasant
Ruffs & Reeves
Moor Game
Guinea Hen
Black Game

7. Middle Dishes

White Puddings
Pear Pye
Galantine des Ecrevisses
Lobsters
Cheesecakes
Pickled Sturgeon
Blancmange
Gooseberry Pye
Asparagrass
Wild Boars Head
Apple Fritters
Salt Salmon
Musheroom loaves
Apple Pye cream'd

8. Lower End 2nd Course

Buttered Crab
Ragoo of Coxcombs
Fry'd Flounders
Hogs Feet & Ears
Lambs Ears
Red Herrings
Collyflowers & Gravy
Spitchcock'd Eels
pickled Salmon

9. Side Dishes 2nd Co.

Oyster loaves
Omelette aux Rognons
Chocolate Cream
Pancakes
Sheeps Tongues
White Fricasee of Frogs
French beans
Collyflowers with
Parmesan
Black Puddings
Custard
Broccoli
Potted Lamprey
Bologna Sausage
Cherry Pye
Apricock Tart
Almond Tartlets'

As for the gentlewoman's table, her cuisine was growing noticeably French in flavour. Vegetables, previously considered unwholesome, and even fruit were served. Sweet confections began to appear at the end of meals. Hannah Glasse had published her first cookery book in 1747, and it reveals a rich and elegant kitchen. Her recipe for Everlasting Syllabub – a luscious confection of sweetened whipped cream, lemon juice and rind and sweet wine – is still, happily, in use today. Since her table was now so gracious, the gentlewoman began to refine her manners to match. Many books on the subject of etiquette were published for her guidance, culminating, in 1788, in the best-selling *The Honours of the Table for the Use of Young People*, by the Rev. Dr Trusler. If the lady had a blackamoor servant, he was given his freedom in 1772 and went on the payroll. She had several other new ideas to get used to: in her garden she had a greenhouse, she left a visiting-card when she went to call on her neighbours, and she could shelter under an umbrella. His lordship had a flutter on the first Derby, took his lady to London to visit the British Museum and the Royal Academy, paid his bills with the first banknotes, and in 1788 bought his first copy of *The Times*. Her ladyship had to learn to play the pianoforte, and travelled in a post-chaise.

François de la Rochefoucauld, visiting the Duke of Grafton at Euston in 1784, described eighteenth-century aristocratic habits:

> The houseparty took breakfast together, the meal resembling a dinner or supper in France. The commonest breakfast hour is 9 o'clock and by that time the ladies are fully dressed with their hair properly done for the day. Breakfast consists of tea and bread and butter in various forms. In the houses of the rich you have coffee, chocolate and so on. The morning newspapers are on the table and those who want to do so, read them during breakfast so that the conversation is not of a lively nature. At 10 o'clock or 10.30 each member of the party goes off on his own pursuit – hunting, fishing or walking. So the day passes till 4 o'clock, but at 4 o'clock precisely you must present yourself in the drawing-room with a great deal more ceremony than we are accustomed to in France. This sudden change of social manners is quite astonishing and I was deeply struck by it . . .

and so on through a four- to five-hour dinner, tea with the ladies, a game of whist and a midnight supper.

The nineteenth century was a time of remarkable growth and change. The population was increasing rapidly: in 1801 the first census revealed Britain had nine million inhabitants, but by 1820 the total had risen to fourteen million – the increase in the entire previous two centuries is estimated to have only been two million – and a large proportion of the working population was employed in domestic service.

Meanwhile, even before the century began, the gentlewoman's kitchen was assimilating a wave of new talent. Refugee chefs from the French Revolution fled across the Channel to take sanctuary in English country houses, in gentlemen's London clubs, and a few in new ventures of their own: public restaurants. One of them, the extraordinarily innovative Alexis Soyer, took over the kitchens at the Reform Club, as well as the feeding of the Irish during the potato famine, the catering for Florence Nightingale and the organization of field kitchens for the British army in the Crimean War. The French *coup d'avant*, or aperitif, began to be served in the drawing-room before dinner.

A brand-new meal, luncheon, made its appearance to bridge the gap between breakfast and dinner, as Arnold Palmer recorded in his excellent book *Movable Feasts*. Tracing the changes in eating habits through the literature of the time, he shows that Jane Austen's household at Mansfield Park breakfasted between 10.00 and 11.15. When visitors arrived at Southerton at 12.30, the Bertrams were invited to a meal, although Miss Austen did not yet call it 'luncheon'. The word itself was not new: Johnson's dictionary of 1755 already listed 'nuncheon' as a snack between meals, and Miss Austen refers to 'noonshine' in a letter of 1808. Mr Willoughby in *Sense and Sensibility* took 'nuncheon' at Marlborough, and at Bowood in Wiltshire, the non-fictional Landsdownes unusually had a 'luncheon' between one and two.

The timing of dinner was also in flux. Thomas Creevy, the perennial guest, wrote to his wife in 1811 that he had taken to dining at 6 p.m., but by 1822 he had swung back to 3.45. The universities dined at any time between 3.30 and 5.00. Lady Nugent,

Luncheon table laid for eight (Edwardian).

SHEEP-SHEARING FESTIVAL

July 12th. 'Yesterday I returned from a visit to Mr Coke, of Holkham, Norfolk County.

'The occasion for which we were assembled was called "The Sheep Shearing". It was the forty-third anniversary of this attractive festival, attractive even to Englishmen – accustomed as they are to agricultural beauty; and to fine old country home-steads established and maintained throughout ages, in so many different parts of England. The term "Sheep Shearing" conveys by itself but a limited idea of what happens at Holkham. The operations embrace everything connected with agriculture in the broadest sense; such as an inspection of all the farms which make up the Holkham estate, with the modes of tillage practised on each for all varieties of crops; an exhibition of cattle, with the modes of feeding and keeping them; ploughing matches; hay making; a display of agricultural instruments and modes of using them; the visiting of various out-buildings, stables and so on . . . The whole lasted three days, occupying the morning of each, until dinner time at about five o'clock. The shearing of sheep was the closing operation of the third day.

'The number of Mr Coke's guests, meaning those lodged at his mansion, was, I believe, about fifty . . . but his friends and neighbours amounted to about six hundred each day. On the second day, I was informed that, including the house-guests, covers were laid down for six hundred and fifty. All were comfortably accommodated and fared sumptuously.

'. . . The dinner courses being finished, Mr Coke rose to bid all his guests welcome, and express the pleasure he felt in seeing them at Holkham.

'His first toast was "Live and let live". This toast was received with rapturous applause, amounting to shouts of joy from room to room . . . The shouts, loud and long, that followed each toast, echoing through the apartments in this stately mansion, standing by itself in the centre of a rural domain . . . until the sounds died upon the ear, had something in them to fill the fancy.

'. . . When we got in, it was past ten. The general dinner company had dispersed; but of the house guests, a number still remained in the drawing rooms – some conversing in little knots, others seated at whist tables. By eleven, most of them had dropped off to their bedrooms. The few left had a summons to supper in the statue gallery.'

From *Memoranda of a Residence at the Court of London, 1819–1825* by
Richard Rush (pub. 1845)

back from Jamaica in 1805, tells us that she dined at 5.00 in the country and 6.00 in London. The novelist Maria Edgeworth, in a letter of 1823, described a trip to Abbotsford when she broke her journey to partake of a substantial luncheon, only to find on arrival at her destination that her host, Sir Walter Scott, was just sitting down to the old-fashioned mid-afternoon dinner. In *Jane Eyre*, dinner was finished by three. William Wordsworth at Rydal Mount in 1835 dined at one, took tea with the ladies at six, and supped around 10.30. In the same year, the historian Thomas Macaulay recorded that ill-health obliged him to take luncheon – which he found extremely disagreeable. The whole timetable was thoroughly confused. Dinner, it seems, could acceptably be eaten at almost any time between 1 and 8 p.m.

Breakfast, however, was still taken at the eighteenth-century hour or perhaps a little earlier. Dr Kitchener in his book *The Cook's Oracle* of 1820 gives a somewhat eighteenth-century recommendation to 'young ladies' for their breakfast, which was to be eaten after a pre-prandial botanizing walk (not less than half a mile and not more than three miles):

> Breakfast itself – not later than eight o'clock – ought in rigid training to consist of plain biscuit (not bread), broiled beef steaks or mutton chops, under-done, without any fat, and half a pint of bottled ale – the genuine Scots ale is the best. Our fair readers will not demur at this, when they are told that this was the regular breakfast of Queen Elizabeth, and Lady Jane Grey. But should it be found too strong fare at the commencement, we permit, instead of the ale, one small breakfast cup – not more – of good strong black tea or of coffee – weak tea or coffee is always bad for the nerves as well as the complexion.

Formal placing at dinner began to appear early in the reign of William IV – starting with the placing of only the more important guests. Gentlemen smoked after dinner and sat over their wine until after midnight. The gentlewoman now danced the quadrille, the waltz and the polka. She travelled on the first train and wore a mackintosh, her housemaid lit her fires with a match, and in politics her husband could vote Liberal or Tory.

The young Queen Victoria ascended the throne in 1837, and domesticity and the supremacy of the family were the order of the day. The Queen herself had fifteen children and her devotion to her husband Albert was much publicized. Improvements in farming methods, which had begun earlier and included the use of manure and other fertilizers, led to increased harvests and better livestock, and some of the new colonial money was spent on farm buildings and machinery. Life was very much harsher across the Irish sea. The Irish peasantry had welcomed the potato on its arrival from the New World with such enthusiasm that, by the mid-nineteenth century, they effectively grew no other staple foodstuff. The British were suspicious of the new tuber, and for many years thought it unfit for anything but animal consumption. In 1846 the potato crop failed in Ireland, and four million peasants faced starvation. In spite of the admirable M. Soyer's efforts in the soup kitchens, public pressure obliged the government to repeal the Corn Laws and lift protectionist tariff barriers to allow food in for the starving.

The gentlewoman of the time was expected to be modest, virtuous and educated only in suitably artistic areas, and to display her husband's affluence on her person and through the decoration and furnishing of her house. Beyond that, Mrs Beeton's mighty and definitive *Household Management* became available in 1861 to guide her in the management of her kitchen, the conduct of her household and the direction of her servants. By 1860, breakfast had developed into a major meal. Taken at eight sharp, it

Victorian engraving of Pastry Cook and Kitchen Maid in the scullery.

TO THE
DOMESTICS.

The Regulations subjoined, for the general Conduct of the Servants, I desire should be strictly attended to, and the House Steward and Butler is hereby ordered to see them effectually carried into execution.

1.—The strictest Cleanliness, Decency of Demeanour, respectful Conduct, and Obedience to the upper Servants, is ordered.

2.—The Time of Rising for the Servants, will be between the Hours of 5 and 6 in Summer,* and 6 and 7 in Winter.† The Hours for Meals will be,—

	SUMMER.	WINTER.
Breakfast	8 A.M.	8·30 A.M.
Dinner	1 P.M.	1 P.M.
Supper	9 P.M.	9 P.M.

3.—Prayers will be read in the Chapel, at which all the Servants are desired to attend. In Summer, at 9 A.M. In Winter, at 9·30 A.M.

4.—The under Servants (except the Footman that may be required for Drawing Room attendance) are to go to bed at 10 p.m. The upper Servants (excepting the House Steward and Butler) at 11 p.m. The Ladies' Maids will retire to their Beds as soon as their Mistresses have dispensed with their further attendance.

5.—The Number of Fires usually allowed are as follows:—In Winter, *the Kitchen, Housekeeper's Room, Butler's Pantry, Servants' Hall, Ladies' Maids' Work Room, Housemaids' Room, and Still Room.* In Summer, the Kitchen, and a little Fire in the Pantry, for the purpose of drying Glass, Clothes, &c. No Fires to be allowed in Servants' Sleeping Rooms, without special permission. As for the necessary Fires, in Stoves, Drawing Rooms, and Ladies' and Gentlemen's Apartments, directions will be given from day to day, by either Lady Hardwicke or myself, to the House Steward.

6.—The Kitchen Fire is never to be longer burning than *absolutely* necessary. It is not to be lit till 9 *a.m.* and put out *as soon as the Parlour Dinner is served*, and the Kitchen is then to be completely cleaned, ready for the following Morning.

7.—The House Steward and Butler is to be most particularly careful to *see* the Fires and Lights completely extinguished after all are retired to rest, and to *see* the Doors locked, and Windows secured, at 9 o'Clock every Night.

8.—The House Steward and Butler is ordered to *see* weighed, and enter in a Book every Morning, all Descriptions of Provisions that are brought to the House; and all Persons whatsoever, bringing Meat, Fowl of all Sorts, Game, Fish, Cheese, Eggs for Kitchen use, &c.; in short, *all* Provisions that go through the hands of the Cook, are to make the same known to the House Steward and Butler, that he may make his entries. In like manner, *Coals*, Oil, and Wax Candles, he is to *see* weighed, and duly entered in his Book, on the day of their arrival.

9.—The Housekeeper, in like manner, will enter in a Book, which she must keep for the purpose, all Fruits, Preserves, Jams, Jellies (made or received), Tallow and Mould Candles, Bread, Butter, Sugar, Salt, in short, any thing of House Provision that would, according to custom, fall under her immediate Charge. These Books will be liable to weekly inspection by either Lady Hardwicke or myself.

10.—The Chair-women employed in the House (except those at times necessary in the Kitchen) are to quit the Mansion at 6 *p.m.* They are allowed to Eat a Dinner *at the Hall Table*, either with or after the Servants have dined—the question of space at the table may arise. Chairwomen are particularly warned on the subject of pilfering provisions.

11.—*No Servant* is to order any thing of *any* Trades-person or Shopkeeper *whatever*, without the order in the handwriting of Lady Hardwicke or myself, *or* without one of our Signatures attached to an order in writing.

12.—No Servant is to keep an Account Book against me or Lady Hardwicke, with the exception of the House Steward and Butler; and any small sums expended for Turnpikes, &c., or necessaries for the Stable, (being ordered by myself, or, in my absence, if *necessary*, by the Coachman) is to be immediately repaid by the House Steward and Butler.

13.—The Coachman will keep and enter in a Book all Corn, Hay, Beans, Straw, &c., received for the Stable use. The Horses are to be fed according to the work they do.

14.—The Horses are to be dressed, and Stables fit for inspection, by 11 *a.m.* Winter and Summer, and whatever Orders are given concerning Carriages or Horses, the House Steward is to be immediately informed that such Order is given.

15.—No Servant is to be absent, him or herself, from the House, without leave from the House Steward or Housekeeper, and then only for 2 hours at any one period, and that only once a day. But should more leave of absence be required, it must be asked through the Butler or Housekeeper *of Lady Hardwicke or myself*; and no Servant on any pretence whatsoever, is to be absent from Meals, or from the House, after 10 *p.m.* without special permission from Lady Hardwicke or myself.

16.—Gentlemen's Servants coming on Business to the House at or near Meal hours, are to be invited to partake of the Meal; or coming distances, Refreshments may be offered them, a Pint of Ale therewith. *Post-boys are not to be entertained in the House, nor their Horses fed in the Stable.*

17.—The Allowance of Ale to be,—for Men, 1 Pint at Dinner, 1 Pint at Supper; for Women ½ Pint at Dinner, ¼ Pint at Supper. Small Beer may be drank, under Regulation as to time, as necessary, *but not wasted.*

18.—No Ale, Beer, or other Provisions to be given away *in*, or carried away *from* the House; also, no Invitations are to be given to Out-Door Servants, or other Persons, to eat and drink in the House; and it is most particularly ordered, that no Ale or Beer be drawn before 1 *p.m.* or after 9 *p.m.*

19.—The upper Servants will be allowed their Washing while the Family are at Wimpole *only.* Maids will be allowed to wash for themselves. The under Servants (Men) will find their own Washing.

20.—The Butler will draw Beer and Ale at *certain* times in the Day, so as not to be continually going to the Cellars; and the Servants to conform to any Regulations he may make.

All Servants are expected to attend Divine Service in the Church at least once every Sunday.

HARDWICKE.

* 1st April to 31st October.   † Winter, from the 1st November to the 31st March.

was preceded by family prayers at which the attendance of the entire household was mandatory. Guests no longer dropped in. Mrs Beeton's first edition did not contain large menus for breakfast but subsequent editions soon put this right. The 'typical English breakfast', as it has since become known, was now the norm in the manor house. It was a meal for which the menu still remains popular, and consisted of three or four courses: porridge and cereal, a fish dish, bacon and eggs, toast and muffins with butter and marmalade.

Luncheon was still primarily a meal for the ladies, although businessmen began to take it up as a focus to their working day. In the nursery, dinner was still served at one o'clock, but the rest of the family would partake of the same joint and called it lunch. When dinner in the middle of the day was the only serious meal, it could be moved at will, and before the nineteenth century, the day had been neatly divided into halves – morning (before dinner) and evening (after dinner). The Victorians divided it into quarters: morning (post breakfast), afternoon (post lunch), early evening (post tea), and evening (post dinner).

The gentlewoman had by now discovered the pleasures and entertainment value of the formal dinner party. She sent out invitations for eight o'clock dinner and her guest list was expanding. Mrs Beeton, ever the barometer of fashion, gave 251 dinner menus in her 1861 cookbook. Coping with a large number of guests, even with the considerable staff now employed at the manor, posed logistical problems. Carving and serving on the long dining table was no longer practicable, and the mistress of the household introduced 'service à la Russe', a method by which servants dispensed food from a large buffet to guests formally seated at tables. Supper had by now largely been dispensed with, unless it was taken as a light meal after the theatre or a snack in the evening after Sunday luncheon.

Yet another meal appeared to bridge the gap between luncheon and dinner – that of afternoon tea. (It would seem that the English stomach demanded nourishment every four or five hours.) A contemporary Duchess of Bedford and a Duchess of Rutland have both been credited as the instigators of tea, although more probably it began as a light nursery snack to finish the day for the children after their substantial noontime dinner. The high Victorian era is well-summarized in the words, quoted by Arnold Palmer, of an old woman speaking in 1944 but whose memory reached back to 1867:

> Sunday was a great day. Breakfast 8.45 for the breadwinner's sake. At 1.30, hot dinner – joint, fruit tart and custard and (best of all) dessert after, the table being cleared and finger-bowls put on, with apples, nuts or oranges according to season. Then came afternoon tea in the dining-room at 4.30 and cold supper at eight. This ended Sunday. The invitations to dinner parties were not later than 7.30, and very often seven. The old maid who now looks after me went out to service when she was twelve years of age. Her recollections are a *good* breakfast at eight, High Tea with fish or meat at five, and cake and cocoa at nine.

VICTORIAN DINNER PARTY

'I will be minute for once, and give you all the *little* details of a London dinner, and they are all precisely alike. We arrived at Cavendish Square a quarter before seven and were shown into a semi-library on the same floor with the dining-room. The servants take your cloak, and I am never shown into a room as with us, and never into a chamber or bedroom . . .

(The hostess:) 'At table she helped us to the fish (cod, garnished round with smelts) and insisted on carving the turkey herself, which did extremely well. By the way, I observe they never carve the breast of a turkey *longitudinally* as we do, but in short slices, a little diagonally from the centre. This makes many more slices and quite large enough where there are so many other dishes. The four *entree* dishes are always placed on the table when we sit down, according to our old fashion, and not one by one. They have them warmed with hot water, so that they keep hot while the soup and fish are eaten. Turkey, even boiled turkey, is brought on *after* the *entrees*, mutton (a saddle always) or venison, with a pheasant or partridges. With the roast is always put on the *sweets* as they are called, as the term dessert seems restricted to the last course of fruits. During the dinner there are always long strips of damask all round the table which are removed before the dessert is put on, and there is no brushing of crumbs. You may not care for all this, but the housekeepers may.'

From the young American diplomatic wife, Elisabeth Davis
Bancroft's *Letters From England* 10.Jan.1847

The Victorian lady had a veritable cornucopia of innovations and inventions to accommodate. She wore a crinoline whose petticoat might take a whole day to iron. After 1854 her sewing maid had one of the first sewing machines. She had envelopes and stamps for her correspondence. Electricity for lighting became available in 1858, although at first she would only have had this in her town house. From 1847 she could have her photograph taken. By 1865 she could sign a cheque and send a telegram to America via the Atlantic Cable. In 1867 she could ride a bicycle, after 1873 use a typewriter and, from 1877, telephone her friends.

Country houses had their first (charcoal-fuelled) kitchen ovens installed in the early eighteenth century. Before this innovation, the wood-fuelled bake-house oven did double duty. Richard Bradley describes: 'a sort of furnace . . . made of Brick Work, furnish'd with chaffing dishes above and an ash-pan underneath.' These were soon followed by the 'open' kitchen range – initially a simple arrangement of fire, grates

Banquet in the Great Hall, Hatfield House, 1846.

and hotplates. By 1850 these were nearly fully-fledged kitchen ranges, complete with oven and water-heating boiler. The availability of coal and iron foundries finally produced the big 'closed' kitchen ranges which are still installed in improved versions in modern country-house kitchens today. The new iron monsters were not easily maintained: the flues had to be cleaned, the iron casings black-leaded, the brass fittings polished.

In London, the pioneering chef Alexis Soyer had his Reform Club kitchen converted to gas in 1841 and gave flamboyant public lessons in its use. The manor houses were unable to take advantage of the innovation since their isolation made it prohibitively expensive to pipe in the necessary supplies. Their gas supplies had to wait until the invention of butane gas in the middle of the 20th century. Electricity was much easier to transport, although cooking on electricity only became universally accepted in the 1920s. The most characteristic piece of equipment in the well-managed countryhouse kitchen remains the Aga. Its inventor was a Swedish physicist, Nils Gustaf Dalen, who had his brainwave in 1929. Dalen was a most remarkable man: not

'The butler is the head of the male house-servants, and his duties are the most responsible, not the least amongst them being the superintending of the men under him if there be several. To him is confided the charge of all the most valuable articles in daily use, and under his sole charge is the cellar. It is needless to say, therefore, that he should be a man whose conduct is above suspicion, as his influence for good or bad will materially affect the other male domestics.' From *Mrs Beeton's Book of Household Management*, 1912 edition. *Illustration from "The Servants' Magazine", 1868.*

only did he produce the blueprint for what is arguably still the most efficient household tool ever invented, he was also blind – and a Nobel-prizewinning physicist.

The Queen Empress and the century passed into history within a year of each other. Victoria was succeeded in 1901 by her middle-aged son, Edward, and the Edwardian lady of the manor was altogether a gentler and more elegant creature than her Victorian mother. The twentieth century was to be a period of even greater social upheaval and swifter change than the nineteenth century had witnessed.

By 1900, transport facilities and the work of McAdam and his successors on the roads had improved communications dramatically. In the country, visits no longer involved hospitality for five or six weeks, but could be issued for the weekend, Friday to Monday, or even Saturday morning to Sunday afternoon. A lady of fashion, the mistress of the house was obliged, particularly in Town, to change her clothes four or five times a day according to her activities. These could range, in a single day, from a morning ride to a midday luncheon party, from an afternoon tea party to an evening dinner party. The entire twenty-four hours had become elegantly and socially busy.

The Edwardian gentlewoman's day might start with early morning tea with bread and butter or a Marie biscuit brought to her bedroom between 7.45 and 8.15. The upstairs maid would put the tea tray gently on the bedside table and pull the curtains. A few moments later, the housemaid would knock and enter with her ashbin, grate-blacking, and kindling to lay the fire; then she would bring hot water for the hip bath. In the kitchen, the day had begun considerably earlier: the kitchen maid had to be down by 4.30 a.m. to start the breakfast baking, although the cook would not join her for another two hours.

Breakfast was sometimes taken to visiting fashionable ladies in their rooms, although the eight o'clock family and household prayers followed by the meal still dominated the early part of the day. Luncheon had become a social event with guests, and had crept from one to two o'clock. Afternoon tea was now also much grander and company would be invited, with attendant maids to pass the fruit, seed and Madeira cakes. Ladies would change for the occasion, and the tea gown was worn to entertain the more informal guests. Dinner settled down to 7.30 for family evenings, and 8.00 for parties.

At dinner parties, white tie and tails were worn by the gentlemen (the first dinner jackets made their appearance now), and long white gloves by the ladies. Senior members were always paired to go in to dinner. Five-course meals for the family and seven courses for company were the rule. (Mrs Beeton suggested eighteen guests as the perfect number for a dinner party.) The mistress of the house presided over coffee in the drawing-room for the ladies, while the gentlemen lingered in the dining-room over port and cigars or even the new-fangled, somewhat *risqué* cigarettes. When the gentlemen joined the ladies, there would be cards, conversation and perhaps a little music. Further guests might be invited to 'drop in' around 11.30, if the party was in a townhouse, when there might be a little dancing to the music of the newly invented gramophone.

Chatsworth,
Chesterfield.

29 Dec 1906

Dearest

How you would loathe this place! It crushes one by its size & is full of smart shrivelled up people. There is only *one* bathroom in the house which is kept for the King. I am going to have a good look at the library tomorrow – the best in England.

Yours Raymond

A shortened version of a letter from Raymond Asquith to Katharine Horner, his future fiancée who he married seven months later. Elsewhere in the letter he reassures her that '. . . Lady Theo Acheson is the only girl [at Chatsworth] and quite nice but not very interesting. I have been a long walk with her in the snow this afternoon sometimes up to our waists: but I never found it necessary to lift her out of a drift'.
Raymond Asquith was killed in action at the Battle of the Somme, 15th September 1916, aged 37. His father, H. H. Asquith, was Prime Minister from 1908–16 and was created 1st Earl of Oxford and Asquith in 1925.

In 1914 the music faded into silence. The mistress of the manor saw her husband and her sons disappear into the blood-sodden trenches of the Great War. Few of the brightest and the best returned, and the great country houses of Britain were never so happy and careless again.

When the survivors came back from the war, the twenties ushered in what was to be the final fling of the privileged few. The Depression of the thirties, followed by the great levelling engineered by the Second World War, put paid to the world of P. G. Wodehouse once and for all. Two world wars had altered the social system irrevocably, and the welfare state now took over those social duties previously discharged, more or less responsibly, by the great landowners. Naturally the taxation needed to fund the new arrangements came initially from the rich. There remain a few private estates that continue to be run on something like the ancient pattern – country memories are long and old habits die hard. However, the hold of these few families is tenuous and comes under threat each time the incumbent dies and his heirs become liable to swingeing tax, or if the family line fails.

To nine-year-old Gertrude Louise Cheney, writing in *People* in 1927, belongs the last word:

> All people are made alike. They are made of bones, flesh and dinner. Only the dinners are different.

2
Country House Menus

The menus and recipes that follow have been contributed by the present-day owners of country houses in England, Scotland and Ireland. Furniture and works of art from most of the houses have been lent to *The Treasure Houses of Britain* exhibition which opens in October 1985 at the National Gallery in Washington, D.C.

These recipes are reproduced as far as possible in the contributors' own words in order to preserve each author's individuality. They are therefore not standardized as would be expected in an ordinary cookery book.

Note: American measurements are given in brackets after UK measurements.

ABBOTSFORD

ROXBURGHSHIRE

Owner: Mrs Maxwell-Scott

Sir Walter Scott's longing for a border property led him to buy, in 1811, a small farm of 110 acres called Cartley Hole. The land had once belonged to Melrose Abbey and lay close to an old ford spanning the River Tweed. Scott therefore decided to re-christen his new property Abbotsford. By 1822 he was in a position to pull down the farmhouse, having already added an armoury, dining-room, study and conservatory to the modest building he had acquired, and build a new house designed by William Atkinson. Abbotsford was never a mere house to Scott. Rather, it was a border ballad created out of brick, stone and mortar into which he poured his loves and dreams.

MENU

Cock-a-leekie soup

The Cleikum haggis with clapshot

Meg Dod's het pint

COCK-A-LEEKIE SOUP

(As served by Mistress Margaret Dods
of the Cleikum Inn in Sir Walter Scott's
St Ronan's Well)

Serves 8–10

4–6 lb shin beef
1 large chicken
5 lb leeks
salt and pepper

'Boil from four to six pounds of good shin beef, well broken, till the liquor is very good. Strain it, and put to it a capon, or large fowl, trussed as for boiling, and when it boils, half the quantity of blanched leeks intended to be used, well cleaned, and cut in inch lengths, or longer. Skim this carefully. In a half-hour, add the remaining part of the leeks and a seasoning of pepper and salt. The soup must be very thick of leeks, and the first part of them must be boiled down into the soup until it becomes a lubricious compound. Sometimes the capon is served in the tureen with the soup. This makes good leek-soup without the fowl. Some people thicken cock-a-leekie with the flour of oatmeal. Those who dislike so much of the leeks may substitute German greens, or spinach, for one-half of them, and we consider this an improvement, greens especially, if tender and long-boiled, and not too finely shred. Reject the coarse green of the leeks. Prunes and raisins used to be put into this soup. The practice is nearly obsolete.'

THE CLEIKUM HAGGIS

Serves 4

1 sheep's (or lamb's) stomach
1 sheep's (or lamb's) 'pluck'
(the liver, heart and lungs)
1 lb onions
1 lb beef suet
6 oz (1½ cups) coarse oatmeal
pepper, salt, cayenne
juice of 1 lemon

Clean the stomach bag thoroughly and soak overnight in a heavily salted vinegar and water solution.

Wash the pluck, put into salted cold water and bring to the boil. Simmer for an hour at least. If you are using the lungs, make sure the windpipe hangs over the side of the pan to empty.

Drain the pluck and check it over, removing the black bits and veins. Grate the liver and chop the rest of the meat. (You may not need all the liver – half is usually enough.) Chop the suet. Chop the onions and scald them. Mix the meat, suet and onions together, and spread them out on the table. Sprinkle the oatmeal over the top. Season well with the salt, cayenne, lemon juice, and a heavy hand on the pepper mill. The secret lies in the proportions and you will soon establish your own preference. Mix the whole lot together and stuff it into the clean stomach bag – which should be a little over half full to allow room for the oatmeal to swell. Moisten with good stock – enough to make the mixture look juicy. Press out the air and sew up the bag. Put the haggis on an upturned saucer in a pan of boiling water or stock. Prick the bag with a needle when it first swells. Cook for three hours if the haggis is a large one.

Serve the haggis with *Clapshot* – equal quantities of boiled potatoes and turnips (the Scots prefer the yellow Swedish variety), well-seasoned and mashed together with good dripping or butter.

MEG DOD'S HET PINT

Serves 8–10

2 qt (2½ qt) mild ale
nutmeg
sugar
3 eggs
½ pt (1¼ cups) whisky

Grate a nutmeg into the mild ale, and bring it to the point of boiling. Mix a little cold ale with enough sugar to sweeten this, and three eggs well beaten. Gradually mix the hot ale with the eggs, taking care that they do not curdle. Put in the whisky, and bring it once more nearly to the boil and then briskly pour it from one vessel into another till it becomes smooth and bright.

BADMINTON

GLOUCESTERSHIRE

Owner: The Duke of Beaufort

The first member of the Somerset family to own what was then the manor of Badminton was Edward, Earl of Worcester, who bought it in 1608. The house did not become the family's principal seat until after the Civil War, when Raglan Castle, where Lord Worcester had previously lived, suffered heavy damage in the fighting. The first Duke of Beaufort (the title dates from 1682) embarked on an extensive building and planting programme; his household consisted of 200 people and needed substantial amounts of space. Badminton was greatly altered in 1740 by William Kent, whose cupolas and pavilion are still outstanding features of his design, and 'Capability' Brown was called in to improve the park. Badminton also gave birth to the game that bears its name.

MENU

Marinated kipper fillets

Roast chicken and bread sauce

Mushrooms in devilled sauce

Badminton cup

Captain Mark Phillips at Badminton for the horse trials

MARINATED KIPPER FILLETS

Serves 4

8 kipper fillets
¼ pt (⅔ cup) oil
2 sliced onions (if small; 1 if large Spanish)
½ teaspoon peppercorns
2 bayleaves
1 teaspoon sugar

Cut up kipper fillets into strips about the size of your little finger. Place in a dish and cover with oil. Add sliced onions, peppercorns and bayleaves; sprinkle the sugar over. Marinate for a *minimum* of three hours. It is really better done the day before.

ROAST CHICKEN WITH BREAD SAUCE

Serves 4

1 3–4 lb chicken
2 oz (¼ cup) butter
1 sprig each of thyme and rosemary
1 small onion
4 rashers smoked streaky bacon

Put half of the butter inside the bird with the herbs and the onion cut in half. Spread the rest of the butter over the breast and cover with the rashers of bacon.

Heat the oven to 350°F (180°C, Reg. 4). Roast for an hour. Take the bacon off 10 minutes before the end to allow the breast to brown. Pierce the leg to test: if the juice runs clear, the chicken is done; if it is pink, it is underdone; if there is no juice at all, it is very undone.

Serve with bread sauce handed separately, gravy made from the bird's own juices, roast potatoes and at least two fresh vegetables in season.

Bread sauce

½ pt (1¼ cups) milk
½ onion
4 cloves
1½ oz (1 cup) fresh breadcrumbs
salt and pepper
1 oz (2 tbsp) butter

Stick the cloves in the onion and infuse in the milk in a small saucepan for at least an hour, preferably by the side of the stove. Then stir in the breadcrumbs and bring the mixture carefully to the boil, stirring to avoid burning the milk on the base of the pan. When hot and thickened, remove the onion and cloves. Season and beat in the butter.

MUSHROOMS IN DEVILLED SAUCE

Serves 6

1 lb flat mushrooms
4 oz (½ cup) butter
½ pt (1¼ cups) double cream
Worcester sauce

Wipe mushrooms and trim the stalks; leave whole. Fry the mushrooms in butter and drain them. Arrange them in a gratin dish. Make a mixture of the cream and Worcester sauce according to your taste. Pour over the mushrooms and put under the grill until they are sizzling hot. Serve immediately with hot toast.

Kidneys can be cooked in the same way.

BADMINTON CUP

1 bottle of Burgundy
rind of 1 orange and juice of 2
1 wine glass of Curaçao
1 oz (2 tbsp) brown sugar
soda water

Mix together. Dilute with soda water according to taste (personally I like more wine than soda). Stand in refrigerator for at least 1 hour. Strain and serve.

BARDROCHAT
AYRSHIRE

Owner: Mr Alexander McEwen

Although Bardrochat was not built until the end of the last century by the present owner's grandfather, the family's connection with the Stinchar valley, where the house stands, goes back at least as far as the seventeenth century. Two architects were responsible for the original building, but all the later work, which included the principal rooms, was carried out by Scotland's leading architect of the time, Robert Lorimer. Although Bardrochat commands a spectacular view, it is also so exposed to the gale-force winds blowing in from the Atlantic that the original owner felt moved to have a Latin motto carved in stone over one of the windows, announcing optimistically that fine weather comes from the north.

MENU

Oeufs Czernin

Roast saddle of hare

Lemon sorbet

An old country house kitchen put to new use.

OEUFS CZERNIN

Serves 8

6 slices of bread
4 eggs, separated
8 oz (2 cups) of cheese, preferably Cheddar
salt and pepper

Cut bread into 6 cm (2¼ in) rounds with a scone cutter (or a cup of the same size). Mix egg yolks and grated cheese into a very stiff mixture, adding salt and pepper. Fry bread on one side only and allow to cool. Pile egg yolks and cheese mixture on to fried side of bread. Whisk egg whites stiffly and form a meringue shape that is added like a cap to the egg mixture, covering both the top and sides.

Place the individual toasts in a wire basket in deep, very hot fat. Prevent fat from reaching egg whites which will otherwise turn leathery, and remove as soon as the unfried side of the toast turns golden. Garnish with deep-fried parsley and serve immediately.

ROAST SADDLE OF HARE

Serves 8

2 saddles of hare
larding pork
¾ pt (2 cups) sour cream (hot)
scant ½ pt (1 cup) strong beef stock
8 oz (1 cup) butter
¼ pt (⅔ cup) vinegar
2 bayleaves
8 crushed juniper berries
1 teaspoon thyme
salt and paprika
flour
juice of 1 lemon
4 tablespoons small capers
2 pinches sugar

Remove meat from spine. Lard well with strips of larding pork. Rub with 2 teaspoons each of salt and paprika. Sprinkle generously with flour. Melt the butter in the roasting pan and bronze saddles on all sides. Pour over them the hot sour cream and add the stock, vinegar, bay leaves, juniper berries and thyme.

Roast the meat in moderate oven (350°F, 180°C, Reg. 4) until it runs slightly pink when skewered. This takes 15–20 minutes per lb. Baste frequently and add more sour cream if necessary.

Transfer meat to serving plate and keep hot. Strain pan juices and add the lemon juice, capers, sugar and more paprika to taste. More sour cream may be required to make 1⅗ pt (4 cups) of sauce. Stir in 2 tablespoons of flour. Bring sauce to the boil. Serve separately.

Potatoes: sliced thin, layered with knobs of butter, salt, pepper, a little grated nutmeg and some stock. Bake in very hot oven (450°F, 230°C, Reg. 8) for 45 minutes.

Red cabbage: slowly simmered with sliced apples, a dash of vinegar, red wine and a pinch of sugar.

Pudding: The pudding must be light. A fluff of lemon mousses in individual pots. A lemon sorbet, served in halves of lemons, garnished with their own tops. Or if, by this time, exhaustion overcomes you, some thinly sliced oranges, with very thinly sliced peel, boiled in a little water, sugar and Cointreau, poured over the top.

LEMON SORBET

Serves 4

4 lemons
4 oz (½ cup) sugar
1 egg white

Cut the tops off the lemons so that they may have their juice squeezed out. Empty out the skin. Take a sliver off the base so that the lemons will stand upright. Dissolve the sugar in 8 fl. oz (1 cup) water. Stir it into the lemon juice. Freeze the mixture. When solid, fold in the beaten egg white and pile the mixture into the lemon skins. Put back their lids and refreeze.

BEAUFRONT CASTLE
NORTHUMBERLAND

Owner: Mr Aidan Cuthbert

Beaufront commands a most noble view over the Tyne valley, overlooking as it does the medieval bridge near Corbridge in one direction and Hexham Abbey in the other. Such a site demands a house and one was duly built there in the eighteenth century. Then, between 1836 and 1841, the Newcastle architect John Dobson was commissioned by William Cuthbert to design him a new house. The present Beaufront was the outcome. Dobson himself considered it his finest country house, built in what he called the domestic, castellated style. For him this was quite unusual, as he is best remembered for the neo-classical buildings he put up in different parts of Newcastle. What he undertook at Beaufront was quite different. In the words of another architect, it was 'a very ambitious Gothic enterprise'.

MENU

Watercress soup

Faisan belle derrière served with
Brussels sprouts and a salad of chicory
and watercress

Redcurrant mousse

WATERCRESS SOUP

Serves 6

3 bundles watercress
2 oz (¼ cup) butter
1 oz (¼ cup) flour
1 pt (2¼ cups) chicken stock

½ pt (1¼ cups) milk
½ pt (1¼ cups) thin cream
salt and pepper

Sweat the watercress in half the butter until the cress is limp; set aside. Melt the remaining butter and sprinkle in the flour. Fry for a moment without allowing the mixture to take colour. Add the stock and heat the mixture gently, stirring until it boils. Remove from the heat. Purée the watercress and add it to the stock mixture. Heat again. Stir in the milk and, just before serving, the cream.

Serve with a bowl of little croûtons fried in butter.

FAISAN BELLE DERRIERE

Or 'Beaufront pheasant' if the above
is deemed unsuitable!

Serves 6

2 plump pheasants
2 large onions
2 or 3 large carrots
2 or 3 oz (¼ cup) butter
1 glass orange juice (fresh or carton)
½ pt (1¼ cups) chicken or pheasant stock (failing that, water)
Optional:
a good slug of tropical fruit juice

Brown pheasants in the butter and remove from pan. Slice carrots and onions and soften gently in the same pan for about 5 minutes. Put carrots and onions into large casserole and lay the pheasants on top. Pour round the orange juice and stock, and season. Cook until tender.

Remove pheasants and carve. Liquidize vegetables and juices from the casserole, to make thick sauce. Return meat to casserole and pour over the sauce, which may need to be thinned with water, stock or a little more orange juice to taste. Re-heat and sprinkle with chopped parsley.

Serve with Brussels sprouts and a salad of chicory and watercress.

REDCURRANT MOUSSE

Serves 6–8

1 pt (2¼ cups) redcurrant purée
½ pt (1¼ cups) double cream
3 egg whites
1½ packets (1 tbsp or ½ oz) gelatine
1 tablespoon lemon juice
3 or 4 tablespoons (¾ cup) castor sugar

I use frozen redcurrant purée, made in summer from about 2 lb redcurrants gently heated with 6 oz castor sugar and simmered for 15 minutes or until the juice has run, then sieved or put through a fine plate of a Mouli.

Whip the cream. Melt gelatine in 2 tablespoons hot water (easiest in a cup inside a pan of water on stove); stir into purée. Whip egg whites stiff with the castor sugar – the amount of sugar can vary depending on the desired sweetness. Stir the cream into the purée, then the egg whites preferably using a whisk. Leave for a few hours in the fridge. The consistency should be like that of a thick fool, not quite set like a jelly, but light because of the egg whites.

BELVOIR CASTLE

LEICESTERSHIRE

Owner: The Duke of Rutland

No castle is more deserving of its name, which means 'beautiful view', than Belvoir. The first castle to occupy the site was built by Robert de Todeni, William the Conqueror's standard-bearer. This building no longer exists, but its nineteenth-century successor is still lived in by the standard-bearer's descendants.

In 1816 a fire destroyed nearly all of Belvoir except the stables and the present building was designed by the Rev. Sir John Thoroton, whose taste was much influenced by that of the then Duchess.

MENU

Marmalade duck

French puffes (recipe of 1689)

MARMALADE DUCK

Serves 4

52 oz (¼ cup) butter
marjoram
parsley
½ orange
1 duck
thick cut marmalade
juice of 2 oranges
little stock or water
salt and pepper
squeeze of lemon

Place a large lump of the butter, some marjoram and parsley (if you wish) and half an orange inside a duck. Truss. Spread the duck with butter and then marmalade (rather like toast for breakfast). Squeeze the juice of 2 oranges into the bottom of the pan and add a little water or stock (during the holidays when the children are at home you can even use frozen orange juice). Cover loosely with foil and place in a moderate oven (350°F, 180°C, Reg. 4). Baste frequently, adding more juice, water or stock if necessary, until the bird is how you like it – about 30–45 minutes. If it is an older bird, you may do this in a casserole with a cover and cook it in a slower oven for a longer time. Ten minutes before the bird is ready, remove foil, but keep basting.

When the bird is ready, remove, keep warm and scrape up all the juices with any brown bits. Taste to see what it needs – probably salt, pepper and a squeeze of lemon. You may wish to thicken it, but only very slightly, or it will look even more like marmalade.

FRENCH PUFFES

(recipe of 1689)

'Take a pound of double refin'd sugar, fine sifted. Steep a pennyworth of Gum Dragon in orang flower water one night. The next day strain it through lawn. Bruise very fine a grain of musk or amber grease, mix it with the sugar, as will make it into a paste, in which strew some little red seeds or comfitts to colour it. The rest make up white. It must be rolled till it be about the bigness of a jumball. Then cast it to what Puffes you please. Lay them very thin upon papers that they may have room to blow up and not touch. Lay them on wiars in a cool oven.'

BLAGDON
NORTHUMBERLAND

Owner: The Viscount Ridley

Like many other country houses, Blagdon has had its architectural ups and downs, but as it stands today it is very close, both in size and form, to the eighteenth century original. The first house of which we have a record was built on the same site in the mid-eighteenth century. James Wyatt altered it in 1778, and some thirty years later Ignatius Bonomi enlarged what he then found. Blagdon was badly damaged by fire in 1944 and subsequently Robert Lutyens was commissioned to remove the later additions. In the 1930s the gardens were partly re-modelled by the present owner's grandfather, Sir Edwin Lutyens. Among the features he added to them were a canal and a paved walk.

MENU

Prawn and fennel pâté

Saddle of roe deer

Blackcurrant leaf ice

The Picnic (Lord and Lady Ridley and their children Matthew and Nicholas)
by William Nicholson, 1930

PRAWN AND FENNEL PATE

Serves 4

1 lb peeled prawns
½ lb (1 cup) cottage cheese
3 tablespoons lemon juice
¼ pt (⅔ cup) soured cream
1 cup fresh chopped fennel (or dill) foliage

Purée prawns, cottage cheese, lemon juice and soured cream in blender. Season. Stir in the fennel. Pile into a dish, and decorate with a few prawns and some fennel on top.

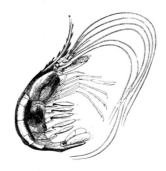

SADDLE OF ROE DEER

Serves 8–10

1 saddle of young roe deer
butter and olive oil
salt and black pepper
4 tablespoons honey
2 cloves garlic, pressed
2 tablespoons lemon juice
1 tablespoon soy sauce
1 dessertspoon (1½ tbsp) Meaux mustard
1 teaspoon cornflour
¼ pt (⅔ cup) port or red wine
½ pt (1¼ cups) cream

Wrap the saddle in a double layer of aluminium foil, with lots of butter and a little olive oil. Roast in a fairly hot oven (375°F, 190°C, Reg. 5) for 15 minutes per pound. Then take it out, discard the foil, and sprinkle all over with salt and black pepper. Mix together the garlic, lemon juice, soy sauce, honey and mustard, and cover the saddle with the mixture. Return to the oven for a few minutes, basting with the mixture.

Mix the cornflour with the cream and port and add this to the juices in the tin. Serve the meat with the sauce.

BLACKCURRANT LEAF ICE

Serves 6–8

1½ pt (3¾ cups) water
9 oz (1⅔ cups) sugar
rind and juice of 4 lemons
several handfuls of the young, juicy leaves from the top of a blackcurrant bush

Boil the water and sugar and lemon rind for 5 minutes to make a syrup. Draw off the heat, infuse the leaves in the syrup for half an hour. Drain carefully, add the lemon juice and freeze.

BOUGHTON HOUSE
NORTHAMPTONSHIRE

Owner: The Duke of Buccleuch & Queensberry

There has been a house at Boughton since *c.* 1500, but the north façade and much else that we see there today were the creation of the first Duke of Montagu, Charles II's ambassador to the court of Louis XIV. This explains the strong French influence apparent in the design of the house, as well as that of the formal gardens that once adjoined it.. Through the marriage of the third Duke of Buccleuch to the Montagu heiress, Boughton went to his family, whose descendant, the present Duke of Buccleuch & Queensberry, possesses it still. The dower house, however, is lived in by Sir David Scott, a grandson of the fifth Duke, to whose wife we owe the following menu.

MENU

Mulligatawny soup

Norwegian pigeons

Buttered apples

The Chef (Joseph Florence, chef to the 3rd, 4th and 5th Dukes of Buccleuch)
by John Ainslie, 1817

MULLIGATAWNY SOUP

Serves 6

2 oz (¼ cup) butter
1 tablespoon curry powder
2 carrots, diced
1 small cabbage, chopped
1 turnip, diced
2 onions, chopped
2 apples, peeled, cored and diced
1½ pt (3¾ cups) stock
¼ pt (⅔ cup) milk
¼ pt (⅔ cup) cream
bowl of chutney (preferably homemade)

Sweat the vegetables and apples with the curry powder in the butter in a large saucepan for five minutes. Add the stock, bring to the boil, and simmer until the vegetables are soft (about half an hour). Liquidize. Add the milk and cream at the last minute before serving.

Pass the bowl of chutney to allow all the guests to add their own.

NORWEGIAN PIGEONS

Serves 6

3 pigeons
2 oz (¼ cup) butter
¾ pt (2 cups) milk (warmed)
4 oz goat's cheese (*gjetost* is a good one)
6 pieces fried bread
salt and pepper

After pigeons have been cleaned and the claws cut off, they should be thoroughly dried and browned in a casserole with the butter, turning them round all the time till they are light brown. It takes 20 minutes. Add salt and pepper. Pour warm milk over and leave to simmer while gravy is made.

Gravy: 2 oz (4 tbsp) butter, 2 heaped teaspoons flour. Put butter in a heavy frying pan, melt it and add 2 heaped teaspoons of flour, stirring for 10–20 minutes till it becomes a smooth paste and golden brown. Then add with a ladle, little by little, the stock in which the pigeons have been simmering and mix thoroughly. Return this thickened sauce to the casserole with the pigeons. If more sauce is wanted, add more warm milk. Let pigeons simmer on low heat with the lid on for at least 3½ hours or till the meat loosens from the bone. Ten minutes before serving, add grated goat's cheese, first 1 half, then the other. Serve on fried bread with sauce poured over it.

Serve with cabbage, rice and a tomato salad with parsley.

BUTTERED APPLES

Serves 6

2 lb sweet apples
2 oz (¼ cup) butter
3–4 tablespoons castor sugar
a little vanilla

Peel and core the apples, then slice them thinly and evenly. Melt the butter in a frying pan. Add the apples and sugar (and vanilla if desired). Warm gently until the apples are pale golden and transparent. Turn the slices over very gently to avoid breaking them. If they are closely packed, shake the pan rather than stir the apples. Serve very hot.

CAWDOR CASTLE
NAIRN

Owner: The Earl Cawdor

Although Cawdor was built 200 years after Macbeth's death, the castle will forever be associated with Shakespeare's tragedy. Its present owner, the twenty-fourth Thane of Cawdor, descends from the daughter born posthumously to the eighth Thane in the thirteenth century; the child was married at the age of two to a Campbell of Cawdor. The tower house was built in 1370. According to Cawdor legend, a fourteenth-century Thane was told in a dream that if he loaded a donkey with gold and built a castle on the spot where the donkey first lay down, good luck would be his reward. The donkey lay down beside a hawthorn tree, and a hawthorn still grows in one of the tower's ground floor rooms to record the Thane's belief in the prophecy.

MENU

Cold lettuce soup

Sea trout *en croûte au beurre blanc*

Spiced steak tartare

Sugared red currants

LETTUCE SOUP

Serves 6

1 oz (2 tbsp) butter
1 medium-sized onion
2 pt (5 cups) chicken stock
2 large heads lettuce

salt
freshly milled pepper
2 tablespoons chopped fresh
coriander

Melt the butter in a saucepan. Peel and finely chop the onion. Add to the pan. Cover and fry gently for about 5 minutes, or until the onion is soft and tender. Stir in the stock and bring up to the boil. Add the lettuce, coarsely shredded, to the pan, bring back up to the boil and then draw the pan off the heat. Liquidize in an electric blender. Season to taste with salt and pepper.

Allow the soup to cool and then chill. Serve cold, sprinkled with finely chopped fresh coriander.

SEA TROUT EN CROUTE AU BEURRE BLANC

Serves 6

4 lb fresh salmon trout, lightly poached
6 oz (¾ cup) butter
4 oz (¾ cup) flour
¾ pt (2 cups) milk
5 oz (1 cup) shallot or onion finely chopped
½ lb (1 cup) mushrooms, sliced

3 hard-boiled eggs, chopped
1 lb long-grain rice (cooked) (2 cups
uncooked)
salt and pepper
1 lb ready-prepared puff pastry
beaten egg for glazing

Cook and cool the salmon trout. Make a thick béchamel sauce with 1½ oz (3 tbsp) of the butter, the flour and the milk. Melt the remaining butter in a saucepan and fry the prepared shallot (or onion) and mushrooms very gently for 6–8 minutes. Stir in the sauce, hard-boiled eggs and seasoning to taste. On a sheet of lightly floured grease-proof paper, roll out the pastry into a rectangle 16 inches by 9 inches. Spread half the cold sauce on the pastry, leaving a 3-inch margin all round. Divide the salmon trout into large pieces, discarding skin and bone, and place half of this on the sauce. Cover with rice, then spread the remaining salmon trout on top of this. Cover with the rest of the sauce. Damp the edges of the pastry, fold ends and sides inwards to overlap in the centre, forming a 'bolster'. Using the paper, turn this upside down on to a damp baking sheet so that the join is underneath. Brush with beaten egg, and mark criss-cross fashion with a knife.

Bake in a pre-heated hot oven (425°F, 220°C, Reg. 7) for 30–40 minutes, until pastry is crisp and golden. Serve hot, in thick slices with *beurre blanc*.

SPICED STEAK TARTARE

Serves 1

1 egg yolk	1 tablespoon capers
dash of Worcester sauce	squeeze of lemon
salt, freshly milled black pepper	dash of tabasco
strong Dijon mustard	1 tablespoon pure olive oil
1 small teaspoon onion, finely chopped	6 oz absolutely fresh fillet of beef or
1 tablespoon ketchup	sirloin, minced
1 tablespoon parsley, chopped	

Using a deep bowl, mix all the ingredients (except the meat and the oil) with a fork, or work them with a wooden spoon. Add the olive oil, and when the mixture is thoroughly blended, work in the meat.

Spread thickly on freshly made oatcakes, which must not be buttered.

Note: A spoonful of caviar on the top of each is particularly good.

SUGARED RED CURRANTS

Serves 6

2 punnets freshly picked red currants on their stalks (3–4 cups)
1 egg white
2 tablespoons granulated sugar
4 tablespoons castor sugar

Take two shallow soup plates. In one beat your egg white to a light froth; in the other, place the sugars, well mixed.

Take each bunch of red currants individually by the stalk. First draw through the egg white, then through the sugar, making sure it is well coated.

Place on a pastry rack covered in aluminium foil in a warm, well-aired place. They will take one day to dry.

Serve in a little pyramid on a silver tray.

CHATSWORTH

DERBYSHIRE

Owner: The Duke of Devonshire

Chatsworth was originally an Elizabethan house, begun in 1552 under the aegis of Sir William Cavendish and his formidable wife, Bess of Hardwick. Between 1687–9, the first Duke employed William Talman to build a new south wing. Some of the artists who worked on the interior at that time were also employed by William III at Hampton Court. By the time Talman was dismissed in 1696, a new south front as well as the south and east wings had replaced almost the whole of the earlier building. After the first Duke, who did as much to improve the park as the house, the sixth Duke was the most ambitious builder. He engaged Sir Jeffry Wyatville in 1820 to make changes that included a new north wing. He also employed Joseph Paxton as his gardener, to whom we owe the magnificent conservatory.

MENU

Sorrel soup

Chicken normande
red cabbage and green salad

Gâteau napolitain

The dining room at Chatsworth

'We always had soup to start dinner when I was a child and I have stuck to it over the years, partly through laziness because it is so easy, and partly because we all like it. Sorrel soup is a lovely dark green colour with a sharp taste. I think it is good with little bits of potato floating around.

'The receipt for the chicken came off a postcard sent to me by my sister Pam from the restaurant in Normandy where it is the speciality. She is passionately interested in food and an excellent cook, and I knew it would be all right if she recommended it. Red cabbage looks nice next to the rather pale colour of the sauce and it needs a plain green salad to compensate for the richness.

'Gâteau napolitain is another out of my mother's book. It can be delicious or rather dreary according to the lightness of hand of its maker. I think it is worth persevering with to get it right. Serve with thick cream.'

The Duchess of Devonshire

SORREL SOUP

Serves 4–6

¼ lb (2 cups) sorrel, picked and washed
1 small lettuce, shredded
1 oz (2 tbsp) butter
1½ pt (3¾ cups) chicken stock
1 oz (2 tbsp) flour and 1 oz (2 tbsp) butter worked together
½ pt (1¼ cups) milk
1 small carton (½ cup) cream
2 egg yolks
salt and pepper

Stew the sorrel and the lettuce in the butter for 5 minutes. Add the stock. Bring to the boil and simmer for 10 minutes. Liquidize the mixture and return it to the pan. Stir in the flour and butter mixture (a *beurre manie*), and boil for 2 minutes. Add the milk. Heat again. Beat the egg yolks with the cream, and stir them into the hot soup. Heat gently so that you do not curdle the eggs. Season. Serve with a small bowl of croûtons fried in butter.

CHICKEN NORMANDE

Serves 4

1 2½ lb chicken
½ pt (1¼ cups) cider
1 finely chopped onion
3 cooking apples, peeled and cored
½ pt (1¼ cups) cream
seasoning

Roast the chicken and joint it. Place the pieces in a dish. Add the chopped onion to the residue in roasting tin, and cook until soft but not browned. Pour off the fat. Add the cider and reduce. Add the cream and seasoning but do not boil. Cut each apple into 8 segments and sauté in butter until cooked – not browned. Add to the sauce and pour over the chicken portions. Serve immediately with cooked red cabbage and a green salad.

GATEAU NAPOLITAIN

Serves 4

¼ lb (¾ cup) flour
¼ lb (½ cup) sugar
¼ lb (½ cup) butter
1 egg
vanilla essence
2 teaspoons milk
apricot jam
¼ lb (¾ cup) ground almonds (sweet)

Rub the flour, sugar and butter lightly together with the fingers. Beat the egg with a taste of vanilla essence and the milk. Mix the egg into the rest of the ingredients with a fork. Place on a lightly floured pastry board, knead the mixture lightly and then cut into 4 equal pieces. Roll each piece out to the required thickness (about ⅛ inch), and cut them into rounds about 6 inches across (with cuttings, there will be 5 pieces). Put these on a greased baking tin, and cook in a moderate (350°F, 180°C, Reg. 4) oven for about 15 minutes. If they brown too quickly, cover with a bit of paper. On taking out, allow to cool before lifting off the baking tin or they may break. Place the pieces one on top of the other with a thin layer of apricot jam between each one, ending with jam on top. Sieve ground almonds all over the cake.

CHICHELEY HALL

BUCKINGHAMSHIRE

Owner: The Hon. Nicholas Beatty

Chicheley was built in 1698–1703, and Thomas Archer, who was employed by Sir John Chester, was probably the architect. The house remained in the Chester family's possession until 1952 when it was bought by the present owner's father. The entrance hall at Chicheley owes much of its character to William Kent, who painted the ceiling.

MENU

Spinach and avocado salad

Filet de sole Murat
Heart of lettuce and fresh pea salad
with mint dressing

Apple brown betty

SPINACH AND AVOCADO SALAD

Serves 4–5

4 handfuls young tender spinach leaves
2 handfuls tender sorrel leaves
1 large ripe avocado pear
juice of ½ lemon
freshly chopped chives for garnish

Dressing:
1 teaspoon made mustard
1 tablespoon lemon juice
3 tablespoons sunflower oil
grated lemon rind

Wash the spinach and sorrel leaves well and remove any tough stalks. Peel and slice the avocado and toss in the lemon juice to prevent discoloration.

Make the dressing by putting the mustard, lemon juice and oil in a screw-top jar and shaking well to mix; add the grated lemon rind.

Put the spinach, sorrel and avocado in a salad bowl, toss with the prepared dressing and sprinkle with chopped chives.

FILET DE SOLE MURAT

Serves 4–5

2 fillets of sole per person,
cut in diagonal strips
an equal amount each of peeled potatoes and
artichoke hearts cut in strips and par-boiled
butter for frying
seasoned flour
2 oz (¼ cup) melted butter
2 lemons
finely chopped fresh parsley

Heat the butter in a frying pan and sauté the potatoes in it. Once browned and crisp, put aside and keep warm. Heat some more butter and cook the artichoke hearts and then add them to the sautéed potatoes.

Dip the pieces of fish in seasoned flour and fry gently in butter until golden. Combine the potatoes, fish and artichokes and serve with melted butter. Garnish with lemon wedges and sprinkle with finely chopped parsley.

HEART OF LETTUCE AND
FRESH PEA SALAD WITH MINT DRESSING

Serves 5–6

4 lettuce hearts
1 lb (1½ cups) freshly cooked garden peas, cooled

Dressing:
1 teaspoon made mustard
1 tablespoon vinegar
3 tablespoons sunflower oil
2 tablespoons freshly chopped mint

Wash the lettuce hearts, drain and arrange around the inside of a salad bowl, leaving a space in the middle. Place the cooled, fresh peas in the centre.

Make the dressing by putting all the ingredients in a screw-top jar and shaking well to mix. Pour over the prepared salad just before serving.

APPLE BROWN BETTY

Serves 4–6

4–5 slices brown bread, buttered
1½ lb apples
golden syrup
grated rind and juice of 1 lemon

Remove the crusts from the bread and cut the slices into four. Grease a pie or soufflé dish. Peel, core and slice the apples, layer the bread with the apples in the pie or soufflé dish, putting a spoonful of golden syrup and a little lemon rind and juice over each layer. End with a layer of bread, buttered side uppermost, and spreading a spoonful of syrup over the top. Bake in a hot oven (400°F, 205°C, Reg. 6) for about 25–30 minutes. Serve hot with *crème anglaise*, a thin egg custard.

COURTEEN HALL
NORTHAMPTONSHIRE

Owner: Sir Hereward Wake, Bt

Courteenhall was built between 1791 and 1793 for Sir William Wake, a possible descendant of the Saxon hero, Hereward the Wake. Samuel Saxon was the architect, and his design combines elegance with restraint. The staircase, which is the original, is also unusual; the walls are marbled and have a cast iron balustrade. Next to the house are Palladian stables built in 1750. The grounds, which were designed by Humphrey Repton, are featured in his 'Sketches'.

Landscaping is still an important activity at Courteenhall, where the proximity to Northampton, a growing town with 140,000 inhabitants, makes it increasingly desirable, but difficult, to preserve the view.

MENU

Melon in curry sauce with brown bread and butter

Halibut soufflé

Blackberry ice
Sabayon sauce

MELON IN CURRY SAUCE

Serves 10

2/3 honeydew melons
2 tablespoons oil
1 onion
1 clove garlic
1 dessertspoon curry powder
1 dessertspoon apricot jam
3 dessertspoons mayonnaise
1 slice lemon
¼ pt (½ cup) tomato juice
¼ pt (½ cup) cream
7 oz (2 cups) shrimps

Fry onion and garlic in saucepan in oil lightly. Add curry powder and leave to cook for 4–5 minutes. Add jam, tomato juice and lemon slice, pepper and salt. Leave to cook for 12 minutes. Put all through sieve and allow to cool. Add shrimps, mayonnaise, whipped cream and melon balls or squares.

Put into glasses for serving.

HALIBUT SOUFFLE

Serves 6–8

3 lb halibut	1 oz (2 tbsp) butter
milk	1 oz (¼ cup) flour
4 oz (½ cup, grated) cheese	2 eggs
	salt and pepper

Simmer the fish in enough milk to cover it, for 10 minutes.

Make a bechamel sauce with the above ingredients using ¼ pint of milk which cooked the fish. Season. When smooth, add the grated cheese. Keep stirring and add 2 egg yolks. Beat the whites and fold in. Put the fish in a dish – cover with the mixture and cook for 15–20 minutes. Serve immediately.

BLACKBERRY ICE

Serves 6–8

1 lb blackberries	juice of one lemon
½ pt (1¼ cups) liquid	½ pt (1¼ cups) whipped
½ lb (1 cup) sugar	double cream

Cook the blackberries with very little liquid until tender. Make the syrup with ½ pint liquid plus ½ lb sugar. Purée the blackberries, then put the purée through a sieve. Add the lemon juice to the syrup, mix with the purée and freeze. When semi-frozen whip the mixture and add the whipped cream – re-freeze.

Serve with Sabayon sauce.

COLD SABAYON SAUCE

Serves 6–8

2 oz (4 tbsp) granulated sugar
2½ fl. oz (4 tbsp) water
2 egg yolks
grated rind and juice of ½ lemon
1 tablespoon rum, or brandy, or 2 tablespoons golden sherry
¼ pt (½ cup) double cream

Dissolve the sugar gently in the water, and then boil the sugar until the syrup will form a thread between your finger and thumb. Put the egg yolks into a bowl, beat well and take the syrup off the heat, allow the bubbles to subside and pour on to the yolks, whisking well. Whisk the mixture until thick, add the grated lemon rind and juice.

Flavour with the rum, brandy or sherry and continue to whisk for 1–2 minutes. Whisk the cream until it will just hold its shape, fold it into sauce and chill.

Serve over fresh or sugared fruit, apple charlotte, and other fruit puddings.

DEENE PARK

NORTHAMPTONSHIRE

Owner: Mr Edmund Brudenell

Sir Robert Brudenell bought Deene, which was then a hunting lodge, in 1514. His family had lived in Northamptonshire at least 250 years before that. In 1566 Sir Edmund entertained Queen Elizabeth at Deene, and it was he and his predecessor, Sir Thomas, who contributed most to the building of the house. Other parts of it, however, were added in the seventeenth century or later.

MENU

Curried crab ramekins

Tournedos Périgord

Chocolate and nut pudding

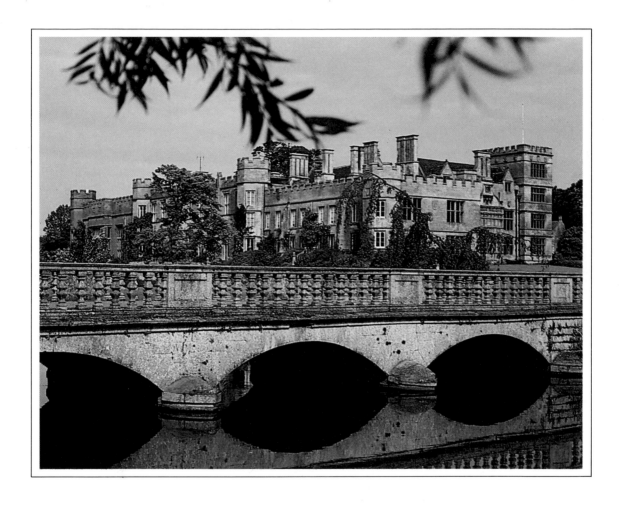

CURRIED CRAB RAMEKINS

Serves 4

1 oz. (2 tbsp) butter
1 small onion, piece of celery or lovage
root or stalks of parsley
1 bay leaf
½ teaspoon thyme
1 teaspoon flour
1 tablespoon curry powder
1 stock cube
¾ pt (2 cups) hot water
lemon (or fresh lime) juice
black pepper
nutmeg
3–4 tablespoons cooked long-grain rice
½ lb fresh or tinned crab meat

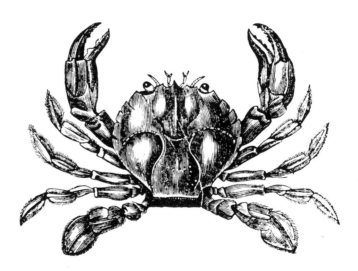

Gild in butter the finely chopped onion, piece of celery or lovage, and the parsley. Add bay leaf and thyme. Sprinkle with flour and curry powder, adding more butter if necessary. Cook for a few minutes and then add water with the stock cube dissolved in it. Bring to the boil and simmer gently, stirring until thickened. Add a good squeeze of lemon juice (or fresh lime juice if available) and a grating each of black pepper and nutmeg. Mix into it the cooked rice and the cooked flesh of the crab or contents of tin. Turn into ramekins and cover with foil. Heat when required in a moderate oven (350°F, 180°C, Reg. 4).

TOURNEDOS PERIGORD

Serves 1

1 tournedos
1 thin slice truffle
1 slice of bread, fried in butter
1 oz (2 tbsp) butter
small glass of Madeira

A tournedos is a round piece of fillet of beef, cut thick to weigh around ¼lb.

Sauté the tournedos in the butter. Place it on its piece of fried bread, top with a slice of truffle. Deglaze the pan juices with the wine and pour over the tournedos.

Serve with *petits pois*, mushrooms and duchesse potatoes.

CHOCOLATE AND NUT PUDDING

Serves 6

½ lb (1 cup) nuts
(at least two varieties chosen from walnuts,
hazelnuts, pinenuts, pistachios, but *not* almonds)
½ lb (1 cup) castor sugar
½ lb (1 cup) grated unsweetened chocolate
1 heaped tablespoon grated orange peel
4 fl. oz (½ cup) brandy
1 level teaspoon cinnamon
5 eggs, separated
a little salt
bread and butter to make fried breadcrumbs

Pound the nuts and sugar together until they make smooth oily mass. Stir well together in a bowl with the chocolate, orange peel, and beaten egg yolks, cinnamon and brandy and salt. Fry a cup of fresh breadcrumbs in butter until golden.

Butter a shallow baking dish and cover the bottom with the fried crumbs. Beat the egg whites very stiffly and fold them into the sugar and nuts mixture. Pour this over the crumbs and bake in warm oven (300°F, 150°C, Reg. 2) for no more than 30 minutes.

DRAYTON HOUSE

NORTHAMPTONSHIRE

Owner: Mr Lionel Stopford-Sackville

In 1328 Simon de Drayton was allowed by Edward III to fortify his house by crenellating it, but part of the hall still in existence today formed part of an even earlier building. In the fifteenth and sixteenth centuries, other important changes were made and in 1702 William Talman (who also worked on Chatsworth House) was commissioned to construct new kitchens and carry out other extensive improvements. These included the building or remodelling of the west tower, the façade of the hall and the grand staircase. The last time Drayton was sold was in 1361.

MENU

Avocado ring with prawns and mushrooms

Wild duck with orange sauce

Cheese beignets

Drayton House by Julian Barrow, 1975.

AVOCADO RING
WITH PRAWNS AND MUSHROOMS

Serves 4

1 tablespoon gelatine dissolved in 3 tablespoons water
¼ pt (⅔ cup) chicken stock
2 ripe avocados
salt and pepper
1 tablespoon Worcester sauce
½ tablespoon paprika
¼ pt (⅔ cup) mayonnaise
¼ pt (⅔ cup) double cream
4 oz (½ cup) prawns
4 oz (½ cup) button mushrooms, sliced
2 tablespoons vinaigrette

Add the dissolved gelatine to the chicken stock and allow to cool. Mash the avocados and season with salt, pepper, Worcester sauce and paprika. Pour in gelatine mixture, combine and leave to thicken but not set. Fold in mayonnaise and lightly whipped double cream. Pour into a wetted ring mould and allow to set.

Unmould on to a round serving dish shortly before serving. Fill the centre with prawns and sliced mushrooms tossed in vinaigrette.

WILD DUCK WITH ORANGE SAUCE

Serves 4

2 wild duck
½ pt (1¼ cups) white wine
5 tablespoons sugar
5 tablespoons vinegar
1 lemon
6 large oranges
10 tablespoons brandy
salt and pepper
watercress
orange segments

Bone the breasts of each duck using a good sharp knife and working upwards from the wing, keeping the knife close to the breast until you reach the breastbone; repeat on the other side, remembering to keep close to the breast to avoid losing a lot of meat.

———

When you reach the breastbone, very carefully come down it, making sure you don't break the skin, ending up with two breasts but joined as one.

Place in a shallow baking dish or pan with the white wine. Cook in a pre-heated oven (400°F, 200°C, Reg. 6) for 10–15 minutes.

While the duck is cooking, make the sauce: Put the sugar and vinegar in a saucepan and boil until it forms a dark caramel.

Peel the zest from the oranges and lemons and squeeze the juice, and add with the brandy to the caramel and simmer for 5–10 minutes.

When duck is cooked, take it out and cut thinly and place on serving dish, keeping hot until needed.

Add the wine/meat juices from the duck to the sauce, season, bring to the boil and add some *beurre manie* (equal amounts of butter and flour rubbed together) to help thicken. Serve separately. Garnish the meat with watercress and orange segments.

Serve with Vichy carrots, *petits pois* and duchesse potatoes.

CHEESE BEIGNETS

Makes approximately 20

4 oz (½ cup) Gruyère cheese

Choux pastry:
2½ oz (⅓ cup) butter
3½ oz (½ cup) flour
⅓ pt (⅘ cup) water
½ level teaspoon salt
3 large eggs
dry mustard
pepper

Make the choux pastry and beat in cheese finely diced with mustard and pepper to taste. Heat oil to 350°F (180°C). Fry teaspoonfuls of mixture (a few at a time) for 4–5 minutes until puffed and golden. Drain on paper towels. Keep warm in a moderate oven until all are cooked. Serve immediately.

DRUMLANRIG CASTLE

DUMFRIESSHIRE

Owner: The Duke of Buccleuch & Queensberry

Drumlanrig was built by the first Duke of Queensberry in 1679–89. It is said that the amount of money it cost him was so immense that he spent only one night there, but later generations can only applaud his extravagance. The castle is built of rose-pink stone in the form of a hollow square, and the architect responsible is conjectured to have been James Smith. Prince Charles Edward – 'Bonnie Prince Charlie' – spent a night there in 1745, and later that century, many of the beautifully landscaped woods surrounding the castle, which are now in their prime, were planted.

MENU

Mrs Jensen's spinach soup

Mrs Rowland's *chaudfroid au canard*

Mrs Rowland's Ripon pudding
or
Harriet's Jubilee soufflé

MRS JENSEN'S SPINACH SOUP

Serves 6

2 pt (5 cups) veal stock
a little butter and flour rubbed together
4–6 egg yolks (depending on size of eggs)
1½ lb fresh spinach
handful chervil
salt and white pepper
cream
3 lb asparagus

Egg custard:
3 egg yolks
½ pt (1¼ cups) thin cream
salt and pepper

Mix together, then bake in a medium oven (350°F, 180°C, Reg. 4) until set (about 15–20 minutes).

A good veal stock is thickened lightly with butter and flour, thickened further with the egg yolks. The spinach and chervil are minced, then wrung through a cloth. The resulting juice is poured into the thickened soup. Add salt to taste, a little white pepper and, if wanted, a little cream. The asparagus (trimmed and cut into thick pieces) and slices of baked savoury egg custard are served in the soup.

MRS ROWLAND'S CHAUDFROID AU CANARD

Serves 6

2 fat ducklings	*Sauce:*
½ lb pâté de foie gras	1 lb cherries
aspic	1 tablespoon redcurrant jelly
½ pt (1¼ cups) double cream	juice of ½ lemon
truffles	cayenne

Take the ducklings and roast them well. When cold, cut the breasts into nice long fillets. Then take the remainder of the meat from the bones and, with a jar of pâté de foie gras (used to be 6s.6d.), pound well in a mortar and pass through a fine wire sieve. Mix this in a basin with a little aspic and enough cream to make it smooth. In a mould, place the fillets and the cut truffles all round the bottom to decorate. Put in the mixture, stand on ice in a very cool place for several hours before serving with cherry sauce.

Cherry sauce: stone the cherries. Pass ½ lb through a fine sieve and chop ½ lb. Take about 2 oz (¼ cup) of the cherry juice, melt in a saucepan with the redcurrant jelly. Add the sieved and chopped cherries, the lemon juice and a little cayenne. Mix well together, and let it get quite cold. Stir well before serving separately in sauceboat.

MRS ROWLAND'S RIPON PUDDING

Serves 6

4 eggs, separated	4 oz (¾ cup) fresh butter
juice of 2 lemons	½ lb puff pastry
4 oz (½ cup) sugar	apricot jam

Mix together the egg yolks, lemon juice, sugar and butter in a saucepan. Heat and stir well till thick, but do *not* boil. Allow to cool. Line a pudding dish with puff pastry, cover this with a thin layer of apricot jam, and then put the mixture on top. Bake in the oven (400°F, 200°C, Reg. 6 for 20 minutes), then put whipped whites on top and brown in oven for a few minutes.

HARRIET'S JUBILEE SOUFFLE

Serves 6

¼ oz (½ tbsp) isinglass
1 pt (2½ cups) milk
3 egg yolks
sugar to taste
apricot jam
¼ pt (⅔ cup) cream
grated chocolate

Dissolve the isinglass in the milk; bring to the boil. Beat the egg yolks and pour the boiling milk on them. Add sugar to taste and leave to set and cool. When just about setting, place it into a small soufflé dish lined with a layer of apricot jam at the bottom. Just before sending to table, whip the cream and put on the top. Sift over a little grated chocolate to give it the appearance of having been baked.

———

EASTON NESTON

NORTHAMPTONSHIRE

Owner: The Lord Hesketh

Easton Neston was built *c.* 1685–95 for Sir William Fermor by Sir Christopher Wren, and was remodelled *c.* 1700–1702 by his assistant, Nicholas Hawksmoor, whose only surviving country house this is. Although the exterior of the building is virtually unchanged, the interior of the ground floor has been greatly altered in the course of the last hundred years. When the last Earl of Pomfret died, unmarried, in 1867, Easton Neston passed to his sister, who married Sir Thomas Hesketh in 1846. Their descendant, the third Lord Hesketh, is the present owner.

MENU

Mozzarella with tomato sauce

Steamed fish Chinese style

Ginger biscuit pudding

MOZZARELLA WITH TOMATO SAUCE

Serves 6

6 thick slices mozzarella
6 slices French bread

Sauce:
1 teaspoon tomato purée
½ oz (1 tbsp) butter
1 tin tomatoes (14 oz, medium)
1 medium onion
1 clove garlic, crushed
mixed herbs
salt and pepper
2 tablespoons red wine

Deep fry the French bread. When cool, place cheese on top. Finely chop the onion and tomatoes. Gently cook the onion in a pan with butter. Add the tomato purée, tomatoes, wine, garlic and seasonings and simmer gently for 15 minutes. Place the bread and cheese under grill till melted. Serve heated sauce separately.

STEAMED FISH CHINESE STYLE

Serves 6

2 lb thick white fish (bass or turbot)
1 teaspoon sea salt
1 teaspoon sugar
1 teaspoon sesame oil
1 tablespoon soy sauce (Kikoman)
8 slices ginger
2 large cloves garlic (sliced)
4 large spring onions (cut in slivers)

Sauce:
2 tablespoons dry vermouth
1 tablespoon sunflower oil
½ tablespoon sesame oil
2 tablespoons soy sauce (Kikoman)

Skin the fish. Rub salt, sugar, sesame oil and soy sauce on the fish. On oiled foil, put 4 slices of ginger, 1 sliced clove, 1 spring onion. Lay the fish on this, putting the rest of the ginger, garlic and spring onion on top (keeping 2 spring onions for garnish). Wrap foil securely. Bring water to the boil in a steamer and then lay foil parcel in the top of the steamer. Steam steadily for about 30 minutes. Mix sauce ingredients together. When the fish is cooked, add its juices to the sauce and simmer it. Scrape off the ginger, garlic and spring onions from the fish, and place it on a hot dish. Pour the heated sauce over and scatter the fresh spring onions on top.

GINGER BISCUIT PUDDING

Serves 6

¾ pt (2 cups) cream
2 fl. oz (¼ cup) dark rum
1 large packet ginger biscuits
fresh fruit

Whip cream adding rum. On a round dish, place a circle of biscuits. Spread a layer of cream on this, followed by another layer of biscuits. Cover the sides (inside and out) with cream. Leave in a refrigerator for 12 hours or longer.

Before serving, place fruit decoratively on the biscuits (Chinese gooseberries, pineapple, pears and grapes go well) and in the centre.

EATON HALL

CHESHIRE

Owner: The Duke of Westminster

The present Eaton Hall was designed by the architects Farrington, Dennys & Fisher and the work was completed in 1974, this being almost the only great country house built in a contemporary style during the last twenty years. It replaced the 'Wagnerian palace' commissioned by the first Duke of Westminster in Victorian times, of which Alfred Waterhouse was the architect. This building was found large enough to serve as a barracks both during and after the last war, and it incorporated parts of an earlier house, which formed another link in an architectural chain going back to 1673. This was when the Grosvenors first built a house at Eaton, although their connection with the area goes back to the sixteenth century.

MENU

Smoked haddock and avocado *au gratin*

Breasts of chicken with apricot

and mushroom stuffing

Geranium leaf *granita*

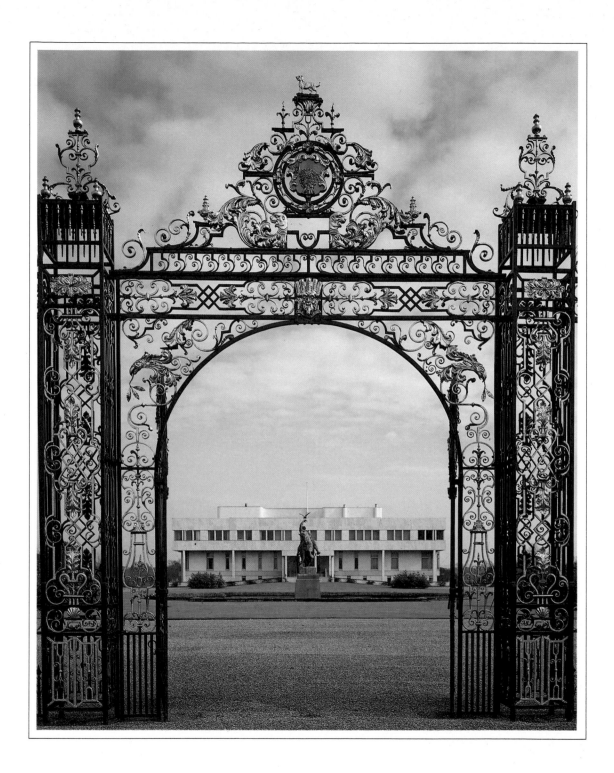

SMOKED HADDOCK
AND AVOCADO AU GRATIN

Serves 6

1 lb smoked haddock filet
1 pt (2½ cups) milk
1¼ pt (3 cups) cheese sauce
2 medium avocados, peeled and sliced
3 oz (3 tbsp) grated mature cheese
Parmesan cheese

Poach the fish in the milk. When cooked, drain the fish, reserving the cooking liquid.

With the addition of the cooking liquid, make the cheese sauce. Mix the cooked fish with ¾ pt (2 cups) cheese sauce, folding it in carefully. Put the fish mixture into an ovenproof dish and lay the avocado slices across the top. Cover this with the remaining cheese sauce. Sprinkle with grated cheese and a few shakes of Parmesan cheese (this will aid browning). Place in a hot oven until golden brown and bubbling around the edges.

BREASTS OF CHICKEN WITH
APRICOT AND MUSHROOM STUFFING

Serves 4

2 chicken breasts
2 oz (½ cup) chopped onions
livers from the chicken
3 oz flat mushrooms
12 oz (1½ cups) butter
1 egg white
Worcester sauce
3–4 oz (2½ cups) white breadcrumbs
6–8 dried apricots, stoned
sprig of tarragon

Remove the breasts from a good-sized chicken, leaving them attached by the skin at the middle; this will form a cavity down the centre. Fry the onions, livers and mushrooms in 2 oz (¼ cup) of the butter. When cooked, mince or put through a food processor to make a pâté. Add the egg white, seasoning, a shake of Worcester sauce and the breadcrumbs. Blend to make a thick pâté.

Place the apricots down the centre cavity of the chicken breasts, overlapping slightly. Spread a layer of the mushroom pâté on top of the apricots about ½ inch deep and sprinkle a little chopped tarragon on top. Fold the breasts together to form a long roll and tie with string several times along the length. Place in a roasting bag with the remaining butter and tie the bag with string.

Place in a roasting tray and cook in a moderate oven (350°F, 180°C, Reg. 4) for 1 hour, ensuring that the chicken is immersed in the hot butter at all times. Remove from the oven and allow the chicken to rest for 15 minutes, immersed in the butter.

Remove the chicken from the bag, carve and serve with a mushroom and brandy sauce.

Mushroom and brandy sauce: Cook several flat mushrooms in ½ pint (1 cup) good chicken stock with half a finely chopped onion until cooked. Liquidize to a smooth sauce. Add cream and brandy to taste, correct the seasoning and serve.

GERANIUM LEAF GRANITA

Serves 6

½ pt measuring jug (1 cup) of scented geranium leaves
(pick only the young tender leaves)
½ lb granulated sugar (1 cup)
juice of 6 lemons
1 pt (2½ cups) water

Boil the sugar and water together to form a light syrup. While the syrup is still hot, throw in the geranium leaves and leave to cool. Strain the juice through a fine sieve and press to extract as much juice as possible. Put in a freezer, stirring every 20 minutes until the granita is formed. Decorate each serving with a geranium flower and a *langue de chat*.

GLAMIS CASTLE

ANGUS

Owner: The Earl of Strathmore

The first Earl of Strathmore built most of what we now see at Glamis between 1675–87, but parts of the castle are so much older that King Malcolm II is thought to have been murdered there in 1034. When Lady Glamis was burned as a witch in 1537 by her vindictive sovereign James V, the castle was forfeited to the Crown but subsequently restored to her son. The Old Chevalier visited Glamis during the rising of 1715 and, in more recent times, it was the childhood home of the Queen Mother, a daughter of the fourteenth Earl of Strathmore.

MENU

Eggs *au gratin*
or
Egg cutlets

Glamis grape *brulée*

EGGS AU GRATIN

This is an excellent starter or supper dish,
often used at Glamis.

Serves 4

8 chopped hard-boiled eggs

Cheese sauce:
2 oz (¼ cup) butter
2 oz (½ cup) flour
1 teaspoon mustard
1 pt (2½ cups) milk
6 oz (1½ cups) grated cheese
parsley

Melt the butter over a gentle heat. Add the flour and mustard and stir to cook the flour. Gradually add the milk and bring to the boil. Cook for a few minutes, stirring continuously. Remove from the heat and add half the cheese. Pour this mixture over the chopped eggs. Sprinkle with the remaining cheese and place under a pre-heated hot grill until bubbly and brown. Just before serving, decorate with chopped parsley.

EGG CUTLETS

(a favourite of Lord Glamis!)

Serves 4

8 hard-boiled eggs, chopped
2 oz (¼ cup) butter
2 oz (½ cup) flour
½ pt (1¼ cups) milk
seasoned flour
breadcrumbs
beaten egg

Melt the butter over a low heat. Stir in the flour and cook for a few minutes. Gradually add the milk, stirring continuously with a wooden spoon. When the sauce boils, remove from the heat and mix with the chopped hard-boiled eggs. Turn the mixture on to a floured board and form into cutlets. Brush each one with beaten egg and coat with breadcrumbs. Fry gently in hot oil until golden.

GLAMIS GRAPE BRULEE

'This delicious pudding is a favourite when the
grapes are ripe in the greenhouses at the castle,
and is also a favourite of Queen Elizabeth the
Queen Mother on visits to Glamis.'
Lady Strathmore

Serves 4

Peel and de-seed about 1 lb of grapes and place them in a fireproof flan dish. Whip
double cream and cover the grapes. Place the dish in the refrigerator for 2 or 3 hours to
stiffen the cream.

Sprinkle 3 tablespoons of Demerara sugar over the grape-and-cream mixture and
place under a hot grill just long enough to caramelize the sugar. Turn the dish around
if necessary, to ensure that all the sugar is caramelized evenly.

Immediately replace in the refrigerator and leave for at least 3 hours until the cream
is firm.

GLYNDEBOURNE
SUSSEX

Owner: Sir George Christie

Glyndebourne is unique, the only opera-cum-country house in this or any other country. It has belonged to the Christie family for over 400 years and succeeding generations have altered and adapted the building to their changing needs. In 1876 Ewen Christian was commissioned to enlarge the house, and this he did in the style we call Victorian Tudor. Some 50 years later Mr John Christie built a music room with Edward Warre as his architect. He used him again a few years later when he and his wife, Audrey, decided to make Glyndebourne a more ambitious musical centre by building an opera house as well. The lawns and gardens around the house, set as they are in a green Sussex landscape, are admirably suited to a summer opera season with picnics enjoyed between the acts.

MENU

Cucumber mousse

Mrs Lott's pheasant casserole

Cheese sablés

CUCUMBER MOUSSE

Serves 6–8

1 cucumber
salt
8 oz (1 cup) fresh cream cheese (or sieved cottage cheese)
¼ pt (½ cup) mayonnaise
¼ pt (⅔ cup) chicken stock
½ oz (1 tbsp) powdered gelatine
freshly milled pepper
¼ pt (⅔ cup) double cream
dash of wine vinegar or lemon juice
1 tablespoon chopped chives

Peel the cucumber and cut in half lengthwise. Remove the inner seeds and dice the cucumber flesh. Sprinkle with salt and leave for one hour. Drain well in a sieve and press gently to remove all the moisture. Dry the cucumber in a cloth.

Place the cream (or cottage) cheese in a mixing basin and beat until smooth. Add the mayonnaise and beat or whisk the two together to get a smooth mixture. Measure half the chicken stock into a saucepan and sprinkle in the gelatine. Allow to soak for a few minutes, then stir over low heat and add the remaining stock. Stir into the cheese mixture. Add a good seasoning of freshly milled pepper, the cucumber and chives. Allow to stand until the mixture is beginning to thicken and shows signs of setting. Lightly whip the cream and fold into the mixture.

Serve with French bread and butter.

MRS LOTT'S PHEASANT CASSEROLE

Serves 6–8

2 pheasants (it doesn't matter how old)
2 medium onions, cut into rings and lightly fried
6–8 oz (1 cup) mushrooms
6–8 peeled tomatoes, or a tin of them
6–8 oz good streaky bacon, chopped
1 or 2 average-sized cooking apples,
peeled, cored and sliced into 8 sections
1 dessertspoon (2 tbsp) redcurrant jelly
a good squeeze of lemon juice
a few carrots cut in rounds and parboiled
½ cup chopped parsley if available
(if not, at least 3 good pinches of dried parsley)

Wash, dry, season and flour the pheasants. Fry in butter or oil to seal and slightly brown them. Put into casserole, add the onion rings, then add the mushrooms, tomatoes, bacon and the apples.

Partly cover with water, add more seasoning as required and a pinch of herbs. Bring slowly to the boil, then simmer slowly for 1½ hours. Take off the heat and let cool. When the casserole is cold, remove the skin from birds and joint them, thicken the juices (gravy powder is ideal as it gives a good dark colour), then add the redcurrant jelly and lemon juice. Pour back over the pheasants, toss on the carrots, plenty of parsley and reheat.

Serve with plain boiled or mashed potatoes, hot red cabbage, sprouts or leeks.

CHEESE SABLES

Makes 30–40

6 oz (1¼ cup) plain flour
a pinch of dry mustard
¼ teaspoon salt
6 oz (¾ cup) butter
6 oz (¾ cup) mature cheddar cheese, finely grated
egg to glaze

Heat oven to 375°F, 190°C, Reg. 5. Place flour, mustard and salt in mixing bowl. Add butter cut into small pieces. Rub with fingertips until mixture resembles bread-crumbs. Stir in grated cheese, squeeze together to make a soft dough. Knead lightly, wrap in clingfilm and chill for 1 hour. Roll out thinly on well-floured board, cut out using a 2-inch (5 cm) cutter. Place these on an ungreased baking tray, and brush with a little beaten egg. Bake in the centre of oven for 10–12 minutes until golden. Allow to cool for 5 minutes before lifting on to a wire rack to cool.

To make in advance: Make the dough and store in a fridge for up to 2 weeks.
Or cut out shapes, layer between greaseproof paper and freeze for up to 2 months. Bake from frozen, adding one or two minutes to baking time.
Or Bake and store in an airtight tin for up to 10 days.
Or Freeze baked sablés, layered carefully between pieces of greaseproof paper in plastic containers, for up to 3 months.

Delicious served with a pot of mustard, as starters or savouries.

GORHAMBURY

HERTFORDSHIRE

Owner: The Earl of Verulam

Sir Nicholas Bacon built a house here in the sixteenth century, and his equally famous son Sir Francis added extensively both to the gardens and the library, the contents of which included his own philosophical writings. In 1652 the house and all that it contained were bought by Sir Harbottle Grimston who, though he was not descended from Sir Francis, had married a Bacon. Between 1777 and 1784 Sir Robert Taylor built a Palladian villa to replace the old house, of which only the ruins now remain as picturesque survivals in the park. Among the portraits at Gorhambury are one of Lord Baltimore, whose son founded the town of that name in the USA, and others of Shakespeare's two most famous patrons, the Earls of Portsmouth and Southampton.

MENU

Pears with cream cheese topping
and black grapes

Baked ham with hot mustard sauce,
duchess potatoes, purée of spinach
and braised fennel

Apple, quince and hazelnut galette

The Cookmaid by Sir Nathaniel Bacon of Culford
(1585–1627)

PEARS WITH CREAM CHEESE

pears
cream cheese
black grapes

Peel, halve and core one pear for each person. Fill the centres with a rounded spoon of cream cheese. Serve chilled with black grapes.

BAKED HAM WITH HOT MUSTARD SAUCE

Serves 20

1 12-lb ham
30 cloves
honey and brown sugar

Soak the ham overnight in cold water. Strip the rind off the ham if it has not yet been removed. Stick the cloves all over the fat in a neat pattern. Paint warm honey all over. Sprinkle brown sugar overall. Wrap the whole joint in a double layer of aluminium foil. Bake in a slow oven (300°F, 150°C, Reg. 2) for 4 hours. Remove the foil and baste the ham with its own juices for the last half hour. Serve hot with a mustard sauce.

Hot mustard sauce:
1 oz (¼ cup) flour
generous 1 oz (2 tbsp) butter
½ pt (1¼ cups) strong stock and juices from ham
2 teaspoons English mustard

Fry the flour lightly in the butter. Add the stock mixture and the mustard. Heat and stir until smooth.
    Accompany the ham with a purée of spinach, braised fennel and duchesse potatoes.

APPLE, QUINCE AND HAZELNUT GALETTE

Serves 6

3 oz (¼ cup) shelled hazelnuts
3 oz (¼ cup) butter
2 lb (4 cups) castor sugar
4½ oz (½ cup) plain flour
pinch of salt
½ lb dessert apples (pippin variety)
½ lb quinces
1 tablespoon quince jelly
grated rind of 1 lemon
1 tablespoon orange peel, finely chopped
2 tablespoons sultanas
2 tablespoons currants
icing sugar for dusting
whipped cream

Brown the nuts under a grill until the husks can be rubbed off. Reserve some nuts for decoration, and grate or blend the rest. Soften the butter, add the sugar and beat until light and fluffy. Sift the flour and salt and stir into the mixture with the prepared nuts. Chill for at least 30 minutes. Peel, core and slice the apples and quinces. Place in a pan with the jelly and lemon rind. Cook until soft. Add the orange peel, sultanas and currants. Simmer for 5 minutes.

Divide the pastry mixture into two. Roll out each piece into thin rounds 9 inches in diameter on a lightly floured baking sheet. Bake for 10 minutes at 375°F, 190°C, Reg. 5. Do not let pastry get too brown or it will taste scorched.

While warm and still on the baking sheet, trim the edges and cut one round into 8 portions. Slide on to a wire rack to cool. Cover the uncut piece with the fruit mixture. Place the cut portions on top. Dust with icing sugar. Pipe rosettes of cream on each portion and decorate with the whole hazelnuts.

HATFIELD HOUSE

HERTFORDSHIRE

Owner: The Marquess of Salisbury

Hatfield was the creation of Queen Elizabeth I's great minister, Robert Cecil, the first Earl of Salisbury, but it was not the first house he owned. As he was the second son of an equally famous father, the main Cecil house at Burghley went to his elder brother. Instead Robert was left Theobalds, a property he gave to James I in exchange for Hatfield Palace. On a new site there he built the magnificent Hatfield House with gold leaf (now gone) on every turret, and imported trees planted in the park. The west wing was gutted by fire in 1835 and the first Marchioness perished in the flames. Her son, the third Marquess, who was Prime Minister for seventeen years, did much to restore the house, and more recently the gardens have been returned to their original splendour.

MENU

Pea soupe (sixteenth-century recipe)

Kidneys creole

Apple suet pudding

PEA SOUPE

'4 pound of beaf, half a pound of lean bacon, 1 quart of peas, 2 heads of Salarey, 4 onions, 1 carrot, a little hole pepper in 5 quarts of water when boile Scumit Stewit till you have got ye Strenght of ye meat Sread a little Carrots and 2 heads of Salarey add a little Spinage boil them together Strain of your soupe and add them together fry a little bread when you serve it up.'

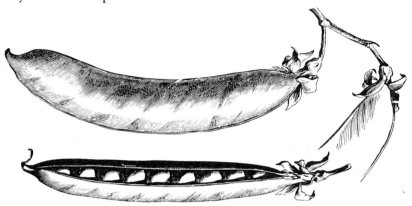

KIDNEYS CREOLE

Serves 4

8 lambs' kidneys
3 oz (½ cup) butter
2 onions
2 cloves garlic
2 green peppers
2 red peppers
1 lb tomatoes
paprika
salt
tabasco

Skin and cut the kidneys in half. Snip out the white core. Melt the butter in a frying pan. Sauté the kidneys lightly and remove from the pan. Peel and chop the onions and the garlic and fry them gently. Add the de-seeded and chopped peppers and then the skinned and chopped tomatoes. Stir all together and simmer for 1 minute. Return the kidneys to the pan and heat them through. Season with paprika, salt and a shake of tabasco.

Serve with white rice and a green salad.

APPLE SUET PUDDING

Serves 4

Pastry:
6 oz (¾ cup) self-raising flour
2 oz (¼ cup) fresh breadcrumbs
4 oz (½ cup) suet
pinch of salt
cold water to mix

Filling:
1 lb cooking apples, peeled, cored and sliced
2 tablespoons brown sugar
1 strip lemon rind
1 cup cold water

Sift flour and salt. Add crumbs and suet, mix with water to make a dough. Roll out and line a greased pudding bowl with one-quarter of the pastry, fill with sliced apple layered with brown sugar. Add the lemon rind and a small cup of water. Cover with the rest of the pastry. Place buttered paper over the top of the pudding and steam for 2½–3 hours. Turn out and serve with brown sugar and cream.

HOLKER HALL

LANCASHIRE

Owner: Mr Hugh Cavendish

Holker was originally a seventeenth century house, but sweeping changes were effected in 1840 by the architect George Webster, of Kendal. In 1871 the building was destroyed by fire, and the firm of Daley and Austin was consequently commissioned by the 7th Duke of Devonshire to design its successor. What resulted was a house full of character, built of red sandstone in Victorian Tudor style. The library consists of over 3,000 books from Chatsworth. Many of them are scientific works once owned by Henry Cavendish, after whom the Cavendish Laboratory at Cambridge is named. Holker's Victorian character has happily been preserved, and the house and gardens both reflect a passion for detail which tells us a lot about nineteenth century England.

MENU

Tomato and bacon bisque

Roast leg of lamb

Damson cheese

TOMATO AND BACON BISQUE

Serves 6

2 lb tomatoes
milk to equal two-thirds of the quantity
of tomatoes when sieved
1 onion
pepper and salt
chives
3 rashers of bacon

Skin and chop the tomatoes, pass through a sieve and measure quantity. Add two-thirds of this quantity of milk, put in a fairly large basin and add one peeled onion (whole) and pepper and salt. Put in a fridge until ready to be dished up. In the meantime, cut the rashers of bacon into strips and fry until crisp, put aside to cool. Cut up the chives very small. Serve the soup in small cups, ice cold, with the chopped chives and crushed bacon on top.

This can also be made into a hot soup, the tomatoes and onion being cooked together in the milk with pepper and salt. When cooked, pass through a sieve again and add more milk if needed – cream too – but it must not boil again if cream is used. Bacon and chives can be added at the last moment (I think better without when the soup is hot, unless served separately).

ROAST LEG OF LAMB

Serves 6

1 leg of lamb
2 oz (¼ cup) butter
thyme
salt and pepper
1 oz (¼ cup) flour

Rub the leg of lamb with the butter and then season it. Tuck in a few sprigs of thyme near the bone. Roast at 400°F, 205°C, Reg. 6 for 10 minutes to seal in the juices, then lower the heat to 350°F, 180°C, Reg. 4 and allow 20 minutes to the pound, with a little extra if you do not like it too pink. Dredge with flour 20 minutes before the end of the cooking time to give a crusty coating.

Serve with mint sauce (made with a handful of fresh mint leaves chopped fine and infused in half a cup of good wine vinegar), new potatoes and skinned young broad beans with tiny onions cooked with them.

DAMSON CHEESE

Damson cheese is one of the oldest country recipes. The cheese, if properly made, is almost black, cutting a deep purple, and should keep for years.

Set the damsons in a stone jar and put them 'in the bread oven when the loaves are drawn' (or, in the modern oven, cook slowly till the juice runs freely, and the stones are loose). Then stir the fruit well and rub it through a sieve. Crack the stones, take out the kernels, and add them to the pulp; this is important, as they give a strong almond flavour to the juice. Put the pulp back on the fire, adding, for one pound of pulp, one pound of sugar that has been allowed to get hot in the oven while the damsons were having their final baking.

Boil well till it jellies and then put the 'cheese' in straight-sided jars, sealing tightly after putting brandied paper over the tops. It should not be used for six months, and improves for up to two years.

It is at its best when it has shrunk a little from the sides of the jar and the top is just beginning to crust with sugar. Then it can be turned out on to a plate, stuck with split almonds, and served, with port wine poured over it as a dessert.

The cheeses were sometimes poured out into deep old dinner plates and, after some days in a dry store cupboard, were turned out and stacked one atop the other with spices and bay leaves between, and the whole pile covered over to keep out the dust and kept in the warm dry cupboard till shrunk and crusted with candied sugar. Such an old damson cheese was a foot high, a foot across and quite hard.

LILBURN TOWER

NORTHUMBERLAND

Owner: Mr Duncan Davidson

As its name suggests, Lilburn Tower was once a border stronghold, and the group of buildings dotted around it are a clear guide to the exigencies that governed medieval life. They consist of a tower (now ruined), the remains of an early Norman chapel, and a dovecote designed to ensure that a supply of fresh meat was available throughout the year.

The present house is by John Dobson, and was built between 1828 and 1843, the work having been commissioned by a member of the famous Northumbrian family of Collingwood. There have been some changes since, as a result of which the porte-cochere on the entrance side, although still large, has been reduced in size. The same is true of the hall and also the staircase which, in its original state, has been compared to the one Dobson built at Meldon Park.

MENU

Cold curried crab mousse

Noodle pie with Jerusalem artichokes

A chicory or, if in season, watercress salad

Orange or tangerine creams

COLD CURRIED CRAB MOUSSE

Serves 6

½ lb white crab meat
¼ pt (⅔ cup) strong curried sauce
¼ pt (⅔ cup) aspic jelly
(saving a little for decoration)
½ pt (1¼ cups) mayonnaise
¼ pt (⅔ cup) whipped cream
hard-boiled eggs

Shred crab meat very finely and beat together with the curry sauce. Add the aspic and mayonnaise. Lastly, fold in the whipped cream. When set, decorate with hard-boiled eggs and a layer of aspic jelly.

NOODLE PIE

Serves 6

6 rashers fat bacon
1 oz (½ cup) breadcrumbs
1½ lb minced beef
1 meat stock cube
2 chopped onions
1 tin chopped tomatoes
½ lb (2 cups) large short-cut noodles
salt and pepper

Cut bacon into strips and fry until golden brown and crisp; set aside. Put the breadcrumbs into the pan to soak up the fat; set aside. Fry the mince, adding crumbled stock cube to the cooking mixture. Fry the onions until soft but not brown; add to the meat. Put the meat and onion mixture in a bowl and add the chopped tomatoes, reserving the juice. Season to taste. Put half of the meat mixture in a serving dish, then the noodles on top of this; put the rest of the meat on the noodles, pour the tomato juice over this to soak through the meat and noodles, and cover the top of the pie with the soaked breadcrumbs and crumbled bacon. Cook in medium oven until the top is nice and crisp.

ORANGE OR TANGERINE CREAMS

Take the tops off the oranges (about 10, or 15 tangerines), making openings only just large enough to scoop out the pulp. Liquidize the pulp, and strain. Grate the rind of 1 or 2 oranges and soften in a little water; strain. Add the grated rind to the pulp and sweeten to taste.

Add some gelatine (about ½ oz), dissolved in water or orange juice, to the pulp, and leave to cool. Whip ½ pt (1¼ cups) double cream lightly and add to the mixture. Fill the orange skins with the mixture and keep cool until served.

There will probably be more mixture than can be fitted into the skins. The creams should not be too set – they are best when the consistency is that of a very soft jelly.

LONGLEAT

WILTSHIRE

Owner: The Marquess of Bath

Longleat, like many another English country house, was originally a religious foundation. After the Reformation, it was bought by Sir John Thynne for £55. Before that it was a Carthusian priory, whose medieval fish ponds were to be given a more modern face by 'Capability' Brown. Longleat can claim to be the first of what Sir John Summerson has called the Elizabethan prodigy houses and Robert Smythson was its architect. Subsequently, great alterations were made to the interior. A library was added in 1690, and at the beginning of the nineteenth century Sir Jeffry Wyatville wrought many changes. Around 1870 the 4th Marquess employed the firm of John Crace to modernise some parts of the house. He also added substantially to the family art collection. The formal gardens at Longleat were designed by the present owner.

MENU

Vermicelli rissoles

Pressed turkey
Orange salad
Baked potatoes
Anchovy butter

Favourite pudding

Reconstruction of the kitchen in Victorian times.

VERMICELLI RISSOLES

Serves 8

12 oz (1½ cups) vermicelli
1½ pt (3¾ cups) milk
2 chopped hard-boiled eggs
1 oz Parmesan cheese or to taste
3 oz Cheddar cheese
salt and pepper
egg for coating
breadcrumbs

Boil the vermicelli in the milk till tender, drain and mix with the chopped hard-boiled egg. Add the grated Cheddar and Parmesan cheeses and season with salt and pepper. When the mixture is cold, form into rissoles, dipping each first into egg and then in fine breadcrumbs. Fry gently in fat till golden brown, or bake in a moderate oven.

PRESSED TURKEY

Serves 8–10

1 turkey cooked in buttered foil
2 or more meat loaf tins depending on the quantity of turkey meat
salt, pepper
bouquet garni
any fresh herbs to hand – parsley, tarragon

Cook the turkey in buttered foil. Allow to cool, then carve it and pack the meat into loaf tins; fill each tin to the top, and then press under heavy weights. Break up the carcass and cook in a little water with salt, pepper and herbs until it is well flavoured. Reduce this liquid by half, and pour over the meat.
    Press again, and turn out when cold.

ORANGE SALAD

Serves 8

2 oranges	salt and pepper
2 lettuces	3 tablespoons olive oil
squeeze of lemon juice	chives or mint

Peel the oranges and cut out the segments leaving no pith or skin. Mix with the lettuce hearts. Sprinkle evenly with lemon juice, salt, pepper and oil, and just before serving scatter with finely chopped chives or mint.

ANCHOVY BUTTER

To accompany baked potatoes

6 anchovy fillets
2–4 oz (2–4 tbsp) butter
lemon juice
cayenne pepper and black pepper
parsley

The amount of butter needed will vary according to the size of the anchovies. Soak the fillets in milk to remove the excess salt. Drain, then pound with the butter to form a paste. Season with lemon juice, Cayenne, and freshly ground black pepper to taste. Add chopped parsley if desired, pack into a pot, cover and store in the fridge.

FAVOURITE PUDDING

Serves 6–8

6 oz (1½ cups) self-raising flour
6 oz (¾ cup) Demerara sugar
a pinch of salt
3 oz (½ cup) shredded suet
1 heaped tablespoon currants
cold water
3 oz (6 tbsp) butter

First grease a 1½ pt (4 cup) pudding basin. Sift the flour and salt, stir in the suet and currants. Add enough cold water to make a stiff dough, and then roll out to a thickness of about ¼ inch. Line the basin with this crust, pressing it firmly to the sides. Mix the butter and sugar together, form into a ball, and place in the centre of the pudding. Damp the edges of the crust and draw it over the filling, pressing the edges together to seal them securely. Cover the basin with greased foil or a double thickness of greaseproof paper. Steam for 2 hours. When ready to serve, turn the pudding into a deep dish so that it will catch the lovely buttery sauce which will run from the centre.

THE MENAGERIE

NORTHAMPTONSHIRE

Owner: Mr Gervase Jackson-Stops

The Menagerie once formed part of the garden furnishings of Horton Hall, which was demolished in 1936. In the eighteenth century, there was a real menagerie on the site, of which Horace Walpole has left us a description, and the building now called The Menagerie was then a folly in which those who came to admire the animals were entertained. Its design is attributed to Thomas Wright; it was built sometime after 1739 and contains very fine plaster work. Recently it has been admirably restored and is in constant use as a domestic residence.

MENU

Oeufs mollets minuit

Sole de Douvres à la Manche

Salade de fruits Clementina

The Drawing Room at the Menagerie

OEUFS MOLLETS MINUIT

Serves 6

¾ pt (2 cups) strong game stock *or* 1 tin consommé
¼ pt (⅔ cup) Guinness and champagne
6 eggs
½ pt (1¼ cups) soured cream
small jar caviar

Make a rich game stock from pheasant, woodcock or, best of all, grouse carcasses, with a little Guinness and champagne added (the remains of the morning's pick-you-up). Reduce till it becomes a consommé that will turn into jelly when cold. If intransigent, add a little aspic. Fill large claret glasses or generous-sized tumblers half-full only and allow to set. If you are feeling lazy, tinned consommé such as Crosse & Blackwell's will serve as a good substitute. One tin is about enough for 6 people.

Boil the eggs at maximum heat for exactly five minutes (this will ensure firm whites but soft centres), then douse in cold water and peel. Place one egg on top of the jelly in each glass. Fill the rest of the glass with consommé and allow to set. Top with ¼ inch of soured cream sprinkled with caviar.

SOLE DE DOUVRES A LA MANCHE

Serves 6

4 oz (½ cup) butter
4 Dover soles (filleted)
½ lb (1½ cups) button mushrooms, sliced very thinly and sautéed
1 wineglass dry Martini
½ pt (1¼ cups) double cream
1 hard-boiled egg yolk
small bunch of chervil

Melt the butter in a frying pan and gently brown the fillets of Dover sole on both sides, before placing them on a warm dish in a low oven. Add to the butter in the pan the slices of button mushrooms, already sautéed and drained. Pour in large wineglass of dry Martini and turn to maximum heat until reduced, then lower the heat and add the cream. Stir, but do not boil, till the sauce thickens and then cover the fish with it. A garnish of finely chopped hard-boiled egg yolk and chervil is a nice addition. Serve with new potatoes and mange-touts – nicer still on Sèvres *jaune* plates with a centrepiece of primroses.

SALADE DE FRUITS CLEMENTINA

Serves 6

a mixture of approximately 3 lb early autumn fruit
1 bottle dark red wine
4 oz (½ cup) dark brown sugar
2 kiwi fruit
½ pt (1¼ cups) double cream
juice of 1 lemon
langues de chat

A late summer or early autumn *compote* of dusky fruits – plums, blackberries, blackcurrants, dates, pomegranates, damsons, cherries – stewed gently in a previously prepared syrup made with Barbados sugar, water and Vin Noir de Cahors, or a dark Rioja. For contrast, top with some thin slices of kiwi fruit, and serve with double cream whipped with lemon juice and bordered by a paling of *langues de chat*.

MEOLS HALL
LANCASHIRE

Owner: Colonel Roger Hesketh

The Hesketh family remained Catholic until at least 1720, for we know that in that year Roger and Mary Hesketh, who bore the same names as the present owners, were jailed in Chester for recusancy. Like many English country houses, Meols had been changed by different generations of the family. Its use has changed too, for in its time it has served both as a farm house and as a hospital. The most extensive alterations were carried out by the present owner from 1960–64, using architectural materials from other, now-defunct local houses, including Bold Hall, from which comes the eighteenth-century cookbook used as a source of recipes for the household offices section of this book.

MENU

Asparagus with Gladys's sauce

Quenelles of partridge and woodcock

Marrow on toast

The pantry at Meols Hall

ASPARAGUS WITH GLADYS'S SAUCE

Serves 4

2 lb asparagus, trimmed
1 egg, separated
pinch each of salt and pepper
dash of tarragon vinegar

Yolk of fresh egg (one is enough for 4 people), pinch of salt, little pepper, dash of tarragon vinegar.

Mix well over warm water. Whisk white of egg stiff. Fold in to sauce – ready for use when it is fluffy.

QUENELLES OF PARTRIDGE AND WOODCOCK

Serves 6

1 lb raw breast of partridge and woodcock (weighed together)
3 egg whites
1 pt (2½ cups) fresh double cream
salt and pepper

Liquidize or pound the meats to a paste. Add the egg whites slowly, beating well. Stir in a bowl over ice until the paste is very smooth. Chill on the ice for 2 hours. Add the cream, a little at a time, stirring until all is absorbed and you have a thick, homogenous mass. Season.

Form the mixture into small egg-shapes by moulding with two spoons. Poach in plenty of simmering salted water for 10 minutes till the quenelles are puffed up and firm.

Sauce:
1 pt (2½ cups) strong game stock
½ pt (1¼ cups) cream

Use stock made from the bird carcasses, reduced until it is well-flavoured. Mix with the cream and heat gently. Pour over the quenelles and serve.

Serve the quenelles with a *purée de pommes* and an endive salad.

MARROW ON TOAST

One marrow bone serves two. Get the butcher to cut them in half. Seal the open end with a flour-and-water paste. Bake in a moderate oven for 1 hour (350°F, 180°C, Reg. 4).
Serve the marrow scooped out on to hot toast.

SANDBECK PARK

YORKSHIRE

Owner: The Earl of Scarbrough

James Paine was the architect of Sandbeck, and it was in 1757 that he was commissioned to transform what was then a seventeenth-century manor house into a building both elegant and more modern. In both aims he was successful, but to the then Earl, Sandbeck could never be more than a secondary house when compared with Lumley Castle, his ancestral seat in Durham.

MENU

Leek and potato soup

Smoked haddock in pastry

Devils on horseback

The dining room at Sandbeck Park

LEEK AND POTATO SOUP

Serves 6

1 lb leeks
1 oz (2 tbsp) butter
1 lb potatoes
1 oz (4 tbsp) flour
2 pts (5 cups) good chicken stock
small carton (½ cup) cream

Slice the leeks into half-inch rings and wash thoroughly – leeks are always very earthy. Melt the butter in a saucepan and sweat the leeks in it. When they are soft but not at all fried, add the flour. Take the pan off the heat and add the stock. Stir and bring to the boil while you peel and slice the potatoes. Add the potatoes and simmer the soup for half an hour until the potatoes are cooked. Purée the soup in the blender. Reheat and stir in half the cream. Season.

Float a spoonful of the rest of the cream and a few very fine rings of raw leek on top of each helping. Serve with croutons fried in butter.

SMOKED HADDOCK IN PASTRY

Serves 6

2 lb smoked haddock on the bone
(or another smoked fish)
½ pt (1¼ cups) milk
½ lb mushrooms
3 oz (6 tbsp) butter
3 oz (¾ cup) flour
2 hard-boiled eggs
¼ pt (½ cup) cream
1 lb puff pastry

Poach the haddock in the milk. Cool, then skin, bone and flake the fish, saving the milk. Slice the mushrooms and fry them gently in the butter. Add the flour and fry for a minute, without allowing it to take colour. Add the milk and bring the sauce to the boil, stirring to avoid sticking. Boil for a few minutes to cook the flour. Remove from the heat and stir in the cream, the chopped hard-boiled eggs and the flaked fish. Taste and season (haddock can be quite salty).

Allow the mixture to cool while you roll out the pastry into a large square, about a quarter of an inch thick. Lay the pastry on a greased baking tin. Pile the fish mixture on to the middle of the pastry, then wet the edges to make them stick. Fold the four corners up over the filling. Seal the edges, leaving a hole in the top for the steam to escape. Bake for 45 minutes at 400°F, 200°C, Reg. 6 until the pastry is well-risen and golden.

Serve with small French beans or a green salad.

DEVILS ON HORSEBACK

Serves 6

12 prunes
12 thin rashers of smoked bacon
6 toothpicks
12 small rounds of fried bread

The quality of the prunes and the bacon is important to this recipe. Soak the prunes until they swell. Remove the stones. Wrap each prune in a rasher of bacon and secure with a toothpick.

Put the little parcels under a hot grill until the bacon is browned, turning once. Place each on its croûton and serve, two to each person.

SHUGBOROUGH HALL
STAFFORDSHIRE

Owner: The Earl of Lichfield

Shugborough Hall was first built in 1693 but was much enlarged in the eighteenth century, with Samual Wyatt and 'Athenian' Stuart as the two architects chiefly responsible. Thomas Anson, a founder member of the Society of Dilettanti, commissioned much of the work, and his classical taste played a large part in the development of Shugborough.

MENU

Fillets of sole with artichokes and sage

Roast saddle of spring lamb with rosemary

Gooseberry and elderflower sorbet

FILLETS OF SOLE
WITH ARTICHOKES AND SAGE

Serves 4

2 globe artichokes
lemon juice
2 fresh Dover soles, boned, skinned and filleted
small amount of seasoned flour
4 oz (½ cup) butter
1 clove of garlic
6 thin slices of Parma ham
2 or 3 sprigs of fresh sage
chopped parsley
salt and black pepper
2 lemons

Trim the artichokes and boil in salted water for about 30 minutes till done, but still quite crisp. Remove the leaves and choke, trim the hearts and put into a bowl of cold water with the lemon juice to prevent discoloration.

Wash and dry the fillets and roll lightly in the seasoned flour; shake off the excess and fry them in a little of the butter until golden on both sides. Lay them slightly overlapping on a dish and put them in a coolish oven to keep warm.

Wipe the pan clean and put in remaining butter with the halved garlic clove and toss this about until the butter is infused with the garlic; remove the garlic. Slice the artichoke hearts fairly thinly and warm them through in the butter. Remove them and keep warm.

Cut the Parma ham into 1-inch strips, and chop the sage leaves. Fry these in the butter until quite crisp. Pour this mixture down the middle of the fillets, arrange the artichoke hearts around the outside of the dish, sprinkle with chopped parsley and seasoning, and garnish with trimmed lemon wedges.

ROAST SADDLE
OF SPRING LAMB WITH ROSEMARY

Serves 10

1 saddle of spring lamb with its kidneys
salt and pepper
butter
6 small sprigs rosemary
wine
redcurrant jelly

Score the fat on the lamb lightly in a diamond pattern. Reserve the kidneys. Rub a little melted butter over the joint, season and tuck the rosemary around and under. Roast in a medium oven (375°F, 190°C, Reg. 5) for 2½ hours. Put the kidneys underneath to roast for the last half hour. Make a gravy in the roasting tin with a little wine and some redcurrant jelly.

Serve with buttered new potatoes, purée of carrots and peas with chopped chives.

GOOSEBERRY AND ELDERFLOWER SORBET

Serves 6

1 pt (2½ cups) water
½ lb (1 cup) sugar
3 elderflower heads
½ lb (1 cup) gooseberries
1 egg white

Make a syrup by simmering the water and sugar together for 5 minutes. Pour over the elderflowers and leave to infuse for half an hour.

Stew the gooseberries in a little water, then liquidize. Stir in the strained elderberry water. Freeze. When the mixture is firm, beat in the lightly whipped egg white. Freeze again. Serve with chilled grapes.

SLEDMERE

YORKSHIRE

Owner: Sir Tatton Sykes, Bt

There has been a Sykes at Sledmere since 1716, but the house in its present form was only begun in 1751 by Richard Sykes. The work he then started was expanded by his imaginative grandson, Sir Christopher Sykes, who is said to have been his own architect, with Samuel Wyatt perhaps as his inspiration. The interior owes much of its elegance to Joseph Rose, who also worked for Robert Adam.

MENU

Tomato soup

Cabbie-claw

Gâteau Pithiviers

TOMATO SOUP

Serves 4

1 medium onion
2 oz (¼ cup) butter
1 lb tomatoes (or one 14 oz can)
1 heaped tablespoon tomato paste
1 pt (2½ cups) good chicken stock
½ pt (1¼ cups) single cream
salt
sugar
pepper

Peel and chop the onion fine. Fry in the butter in a large saucepan. Add the tomatoes and simmer till they pulp. Stir in the tomato paste and the chicken stock. Liquidize. Return to the pan and warm. Add the cream, saving a quarter to swirl on top just before you serve it. Adjust the seasoning. May be served hot or cold.

CABBIE-CLAW

Serves 4

4 haddock fillets
1 small glass of dry vermouth
½ pt (1¼ cups) fish stock or water
¼ pt (⅔ cup) double cream
2 teaspoons horseradish sauce
1 hard-boiled egg with yolk and white grated separately
chopped parsley

Preheat the oven to 350°F, 180°C, Reg. 4. Butter a shallow ovenproof dish. Cut each trimmed fillet in half, placing one half on top of the other, thus giving neat, easy-to-handle portions. Place the fish in the dish and cover with a mixture of vermouth and water or vermouth and fish stock. Cover with a lid or foil and cook in the oven till the fish is tender, about 30 minutes. Pour off half of the stock mixture, spread a layer of horseradish on top of the fish, then cream on top of this, return to the oven to bubble for a few minutes.

If your dish is a good looking one, serve from this. If not, lift the pieces gently with a fish-slice to a warmed serving dish and pour the sauce over. To garnish, sprinkle with the egg and chopped parsley.

GATEAU PITHIVIERS

1 lb puff pastry
4 oz (½ cup) ground almonds
4 oz (½ cup) castor sugar
2 oz (¼ cup) butter
1 egg
1 generous oz (¼ cup) flour
egg white and sugar to glaze

Roll out the pastry into 2 rounds, each about 9 inches across.

Mix the almonds, sugar, butter and egg and beat them together. Stir in the flour. Spread the almond filling on one of the pastry rounds, leaving a border round the edge. Place the other round on top, dampen the edges to seal. Knock up the edges with the back of a knife. Decorate the top with a star shape cut in lightly, brush with a little egg white and sprinkle sugar over to glaze. Bake at 425°F, 220°C, Reg. 7 for half an hour. Serve warm.

TICHBORNE PARK
HAMPSHIRE

Owner: Mrs John Loudon

Tichborne Park as it stands today was built in 1803, but a predecessor was in existence in the thirteenth century when it already possessed a private chapel. The Tichborne family has lived here for at least 800 years and the present owner is the daughter of the last baronet, Sir Anthony Tichborne.

In the nineteenth century, a famous civil lawsuit involved the family, when a middle-aged man claiming to be the lost heir returned from Australia to claim the baronetcy. The trial lasted ten months and was the longest ever held in Britain. Although the claimant lost, there is still doubt as to who he was.

During the Middle Ages, the Saxon farmers of Tichborne paid their rent to the bishops of Winchester in kind: beer, sweet Welsh ale, clear ale, large and small loaves, oxen, sheep, pigs and cheese. Every Lady Day, dole in the form of flour is distributed to the poor of Tichborne in a ceremony dating back to that period.

MENU

Artichoke soup

Sea bass with garlic mayonnaise

Lemon syllabub

ARTICHOKE SOUP

Serves 4

2 lb Jerusalem artichokes
1 lemon
1 chicken stock cube
1 pt (2½ cups) milk
1 pt 2½ cups) water
¼ pt (⅔ cup) cream

Wash and peel the artichokes. Chop them and the lemon and put into a saucepan with the stock cube, milk and water. Bring to the boil, then simmer for approximately ½ hour.

When cool, blend in an electric liquidizer, return to the saucepan, season, add the cream and re-heat just before serving.

SEA BASS WITH GARLIC MAYONNAISE

Serves 4

butter
1 sea bass (or any other coarse-grained fish) enough for 4 people
2 lemon juice
2 bay leaves
ground black pepper

Butter a large piece of aluminium foil. Place the fish in the middle of this and score it slightly. Pour over the lemon juice, and add the pepper and bay leaves. Wrap up like a present and bake for approximately 20 minutes in hottish oven. When cool, leave wrapped up to retain the juices until ready to serve.

———

Garlic mayonnaise:
2 eggs
1 teaspoon castor sugar
1 teaspoon dry mustard
1 teaspoon white wine vinegar
juice of 1 or 2 lemons
2 cloves of garlic (crushed)
½ pt (1¼ cups) olive oil

Place all the ingredients except the oil in a blender and mix together. Then slowly pour in the oil while blending until the right thickness is achieved.

Serve the fish cold with the garlic mayonnaise and garnished with watercress. Hot new potatoes and a tomato salad with basil are nice with it.

LEMON SYLLABUB

Serves 6

¼ pt (⅔ cup) white wine
2 tablespoons lemon juice
2 teaspoons grated lemon rind
3 oz (⅓ cup) castor sugar
½ pt (1¼ cups) double cream

Place wine, lemon juice, rind and sugar into a bowl. Leave for a minimum of 3 hours. Add the cream and whip until the mixture stands in soft peaks. Transfer into a glass bowl and leave in the fridge before serving. Decorate with lemon pieces.

WADDESDON MANOR

BUCKINGHAMSHIRE

Owner: The National Trust

In 1874 Baron Ferdinand de Rothschild bought a bare eminence at Waddesdon with several hundred acres of surrounding land. Before any house could be built there the ground had to be levelled and to speed the work carthorses were imported from Normandy to drag the stones needed for the building up the hill. The property had very few trees, so that everything we now see at Waddesdon, the house itself, and all that surrounds it, was of Baron Ferdinand's creation. That there are echoes of Chambord and Blois in the design of the house is understandable, since the architect was a Frenchman, Hippolyte Destailleur (1822–1893). Waddesdon was given to the National Trust in 1957 by Mr James de Rothschild, complete with the finest Rothschild collection still to be seen under one roof in England. Elie Lainé designed the gardens and among the great chefs who ruled the kitchen was M. Tissot, who gave to Mrs James de Rothschild the recipes which now follow.

MENU

Cold Gruyère soufflé

M. Tissot's poulet polonaise

Guard's pudding

COLD GRUYERE SOUFFLE

Serves 4

3 oz (½ cup) flour
3 oz (⅓ cup) butter
1 pt (2½ cups) milk
1 sheet gelatine
2 eggs and 1 extra white
½ lb Gruyère cheese

Make a béchamel sauce: fry the flour gently in the butter without allowing it to take colour. Add the milk, heated, beating till the mixture is smooth.

Dissolve the gelatine in a little hot water and stir into the sauce. Grate the cheese and beat it in. Separate the eggs and beat in the two yolks. Whisk the three whites to a stiff snow and fold them in thoroughly with a metal spoon.

Tie a paper collar round a 1½-pt (2 US pt) soufflé dish. Pile in the mixture. When cold, refrigerate for an hour at least. Serve with hot toast and butter.

M. TISSOT'S POULET POLONAISE

Serves 4

1 chicken
1 onion
4 oz (½ cup) butter
2 or 3 chicken livers
4 oz (2 cups) breadcrumbs
1 dessertspoon (2 tbsp) chopped parsley
1 teaspoon chopped thyme
1 egg
salt and pepper
1 dessertspoon (2 tbsp) gravy

Chop the onion finely and fry gently in 1 oz (2 tbsp) of the butter. Remove the onion and fry the livers, also lightly. Pass the livers through a fine sieve. Mix the onion, livers, half of the breadcrumbs and herbs together with the egg (beaten), seasoning and gravy. The stuffing must be firm but not soft.

Stuff the chicken and baste the breast with another 1 oz (2 tbsp) of the butter. Roast the bird at 400°F, 205°C, Reg. 6 for 10 minutes, then reduce the heat and roast for 60 minutes in total for a chicken of approximately 2 lb (unstuffed). Test to see if it is cooked by running a skewer into a leg: if the juice runs clear, the bird is ready. A stuffed chicken takes proportionately longer to cook than an unstuffed one. Cut the chicken into joints and the stuffing into neat slices. Arrange on a flat dish. To finish, fry the remaining breadcrumbs in the rest of the butter until a light brown. Sprinkle the chicken only and pass under a grill until they are a golden brown.

GUARD'S PUDDING

Serves 4–6

8 oz (2 cups) breadcrumbs
8 oz (1 cup) suet
6 oz (¾ cup) brown sugar
4 tablespoons berry jam
2 eggs
1 teaspoon baking powder

Mix together the breadcrumbs, suet and sugar. Beat the eggs with the jam and the bicarbonate and stir them into the breadcrumb mixture. Butter a 2-pt (2½ US pt) pudding basin. Cover with aluminium foil and steam for 3 hours in a pan of boiling water. Turn out on to a hot dish. Serve with thin cream or a homemade custard.

WEST WYCOMBE PARK
BUCKINGHAMSHIRE

Owner: The National Trust

The house was built in the mid-eighteenth century by Sir Francis Dashwood, a man of multifarious interests who combined politics with his patronage of the arts. He founded the notorious Hell Fire Club, became Postmaster General and was Chancellor of the Exchequer. In the building of West Wycombe, he employed several architects, one of whom was Robert Adam, but he largely followed his own ideas in producing a classical house set in a landscape that embodies eighteenth-century sophistication. For a part of this achievement, the landscape gardener Humphrey Repton was responsible. The house, but not its contents, was given to the National Trust in 1944 by Sir John Dashwood. His son, the present baronet, lives there today.

MENU

Stinko di vitellu with spinach purée

Tarte à l'orange à la valencian

West Wycombe Park by William Daniell, 1781

STINKO DI VITELLU

Serves 4–6

3–4 lb piece of knuckle of veal, bone in
small bunch rosemary
salt and pepper
½ bottle red wine
1 pkt polenta
2 tablespoons butter
2 oz (¼ cup) grated Cheddar cheese

Roast the veal well with rosemary and then pour half a bottle of red wine over it. Put in hot oven for four hours to cook it completely (if necessary add stock). Sauce should become thick.

Serve in dish with polenta (buy 1 packet of quick polenta and cook it following instructions on packet). When cooked add 2 soup spoons of butter and put in round container to produce correct round flat shape to go beneath Stinko. When polenta is cold, cut in half horizontally and put in between grated cheese (Cheddar). Warm for 20 minutes before serving with Stinko standing upright in centre of dish with polenta at base and spinach round outside of dish. Serve with spinach purée.

Spinach purée:
2 lb leaf spinach
2 large onions
¼ pt (½ cup) double cream
yolks of two eggs

Cook the leaf spinach for 2 minutes in boiling water. Fry 2 large onions in slices. Put all in the blender. Add cream, salt, pepper and sugar and yolk of 2 eggs.

TARTE A L'ORANGE A LA VALENCIAN

Serves 6–8

8 oz (2 cups) pastry flour (not all-purpose flour)
6 oz (¾ cup) butter
pinch of salt
2 tablespoons castor sugar
1 egg beaten with 3 tablespoons cold water
4 tablespoons apricot jam
1 cup + 6½ tablespoons granulated sugar
1 cup orange juice (or ½ orange juice and ½ lemon juice)
2 large thick-skinned oranges
2 egg yolks
2 oz (⅜ cup) ground almonds
¼ cup orange liqueur

You will need an 8–9-inch tart mould or ring.

Preheat the oven to 375°F, 190°C, Reg. 5. To make the pastry, work the flour, 4 oz (½ cup) butter, salt and sugar together. Mix to a smooth soft ball with the egg and water mixture. Wrap in clingfilm and refrigerate for at least 20 minutes.

Warm and strain the apricot jam. Roll out the pastry to a thickness of ⅛ inch. Line the tart mould with the pastry. Prick the bottom with a fork and spread the apricot jam over the pastry. Refrigerate to firm again. Bake the tart shell for 12 to 15 minutes until it has drawn slightly away from the sides of the mould and is very lightly coloured. Set aside to cool.

Make a syrup by slowly boiling 1 cup of the sugar with the orange juice (or orange and lemon juice) for 20 minutes. Wash and wipe the oranges and cut them, unpeeled, into neat thin rounds. Add them to the syrup and simmer for 10 to 15 minutes until they are well glazed. Spread them out on a rack to dry, reserving the syrup. When they are dry, cut them into quarters.

Beat the egg yolks with 3½ tablespoons of the sugar until the mixture is a pale yellow. Cream the remaining butter and the remaining sugar. Blend with the egg yolks and add the ground almonds.

Preheat the oven to 400°F, 205°C, Reg. 6. Fill the cooled tart shell with the almond cream and bake in the oven for 8 to 10 minutes until the cream is set and golden brown. Let cool for about 10 minutes.

Boil down the reserved orange syrup until it has the consistency of a glaze. Remove it from the heat and immediately stir in the orange liqueur. Arrange the quartered orange slices on the tart in overlapping circular rows. Pour the glaze over the oranges (if it has cooled too much, reheat it to make it more fluid). Let the tart cool completely before unmoulding and serving.

WOBURN ABBEY

BEDFORDSHIRE

Owner: The Marquess of Tavistock

Woburn Abbey was given by Henry VIII to John Russell after the dissolution of the monasteries in 1539, but the family did not live there until the seventeenth century. Much of the house that was then built was destroyed in the eighteenth century when John Sandeman and, later, Henry Flitcroft re-modelled the Abbey. At the end of that century, Henry Holland added an east front (now pulled down) and a beautiful Chinese dairy.

MENU

Croque monsieur

Canard sauvage aux navets

Toblerone mousse in a meringue nest
or
Blackberry mousse

The Chinese Dairy from *The Red Book of Woburn Abbey*
by Humphry Repton, 1804

CROQUE MONSIEUR

Serves 4

8 slices of bread
4 slices of smoked ham
4 slices of Cheddar cheese
butter

Butter one side of each of the four slices of bread, place a layer of cheese and a layer of ham on this and cover with another slice of bread to make a sandwich. Cut in half.

Melt butter in a frying pan and shallow fry the sandwiches on both sides until golden brown. Serve immediately.

CANARD SAUVAGE AUX NAVETS

1 duck per person if the birds are small, such as teal. Otherwise, 1 bird will feed 2 people
butter
thyme
rosemary
small glass of port
a little stock

These birds should be served rare. Roast them, with a little butter basted on the breast and the herbs and another knob of butter inside, in a hot oven (425°F, 220°C, Reg. 7) for 30 minutes for the larger birds, less for the smaller ones.

De-glaze the pan juices with the port and the stock. Hand this sauce separately with a knob of butter beaten in at the last minute.

Serve with a purée of turnips and potato and a watercress salad.

TOBLERONE MOUSSE IN A MERINGUE NEST

Serves 4–6

For the meringue:	*For the mousse:*
4 egg whites	7 oz Toblerone and some for
½ teaspoon vinegar	decoration
8 oz (1 cup) castor sugar	6 tablespoons boiling water
	½ pt (1¼ cups) thick cream
	2 egg whites

Preheat the oven to 250°F, 100°C, Reg. ½.

Whisk the 4 egg whites until stiff. Slowly fold in the castor sugar and lastly the vinegar. Pipe on to a greased, lined baking sheet into a nest shape. Bake in the oven for 2 hours or until it is completely dry. Cool on a wire rack.

Melt the Toblerone with the boiling water in the top half of a double boiler. Cool until it is nearly set. Whip the cream and fold into the Toblerone mixture. Whip the egg whites and fold into the mixture (this should be almost set). Pour into the centre of the meringue nest and leave in a cool place, but *not* a fridge or the meringue will soften.

To serve, grate some Toblerone over the top. This also makes a nice mousse without the meringue and can be served straight from the freezer as a frozen mousse.

BLACKBERRY MOUSSE

Serves 4–6

20 oz (2½ cups) fresh or frozen blackberries
juice of 2 oranges, zest of 1
1 tablespoon powdered gelatine
3 tablespoons water
2 eggs, separated
1 pt (2½ cups) double cream, whipped
2 oz (¼ cup) sugar

Mix the blackberries with the orange juice and zest and bring to the boil. Dissolve the gelatine in the water over a low heat, add to the blackberries and allow to cool. Beat the egg yolks and sugar together until light and fluffy; fold into the cooled blackberries and then fold in the whipped cream. Whisk the egg whites to firm peaks and gently fold into the blackberry mixture. Pour into a glass bowl and leave to set. Decorate with extra blackberries and cream.

'The serviettes or table napkins should be neatly and tastefully folded when first put on the table. . . . The accompanying engravings depict the designs most in favour and the methods of folding them. It must, however, be remembered that it is useless to attempt anything but the most simple forms unless the napkins have been slightly starched and smoothly ironed. In every case the folding must be exact, or the result will be slovenly and unsightly. The usual size of these indispensable accompaniments to the dinner table is a square measuring about 30 inches.' From *Mrs. Beeton's Book of Household Management,* 1912 edition.

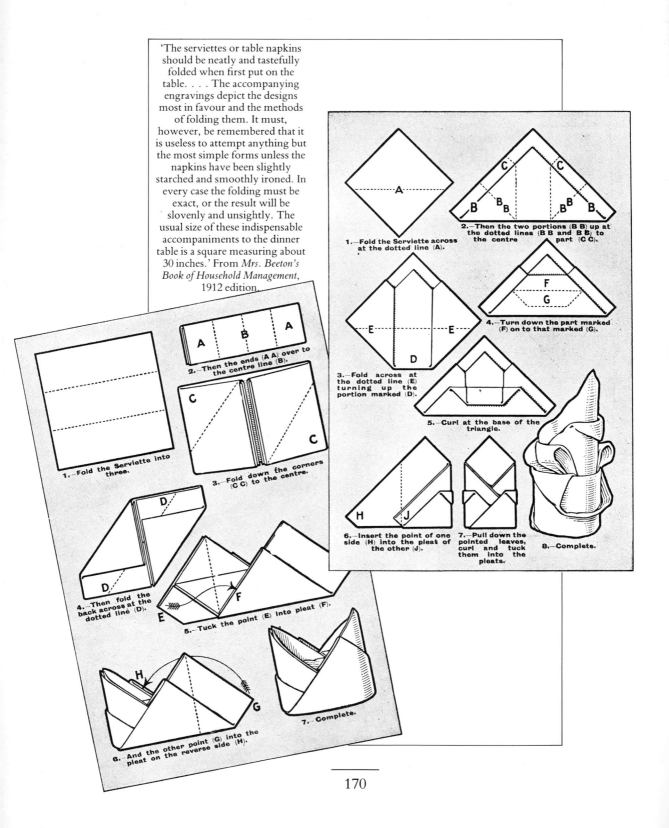

1.—Fold the Serviette across at the dotted line (A).

2.—Then the two portions (B B) up at the dotted lines (B B and B B) to the centre part (C C).

3.—Fold across at the dotted line (E) turning up the portion marked (D).

4.—Turn down the part marked (F) on to that marked (G).

5.—Curl at the base of the triangle.

6.—Insert the point of one side (H) into the pleat of the other (J).

7.—Pull down the pointed leaves, curl and tuck them into the pleats.

8.—Complete.

1.—Fold the Serviette into three.

2.—Then the ends (A A) over to the centre line (B).

3.—Fold down the corners (C C) to the centre.

4.—Then fold the back across at the dotted line (D).

5.—Tuck the point (E) into pleat (F).

6.—And the other point (G) into the pleat on the reverse side (H).

7.—Complete.

3

The Household Offices

Country households have always kept 'household books' – manuscript collections of recipes and household notes made by the mistress of the house, or sometimes by the master. Most of them date from the eighteenth century, such as the Scottish 'Household Book of Lady Grisell Baillie' dated 1692–1733, although some, such as Mary Fairfax of Ashton's sixteenth-century 'Arcana Fairfaxiana', are much earlier.

The main sources for this chapter are the nineteenth-century 'Sandbeck Household Book', and the eighteenth-century 'Bold Hall Cookery Book'. These are manuscript household books kept by the families of the Earls of Scarbrough and the Bolds of Lancashire respectively. Since correspondence about recipes from other households was saved and the recipes transcribed, each individual book also has entries from the household books of other houses. The aristocracy visited, and still visits, each others' houses frequently; each house has its own particular style, and recipes continue to be exchanged.

The recipes given here have never, as far as we know, been published before. They have not been altered, but transcribed as they appear in the originals. Some of them are still eminently usable today, others are included as interesting curiosities. The recipes have been arranged under the various 'kitchen offices' recommended by Robert Kerr in his 1865 masterwork on Victorian English domestic architecture, *The Gentleman's House; or How to Plan English Residences from the Parsonage to the Palace*.

The meat larder

Raw meat for the country house kitchen was stored, as it occasionally still is, in the wet or meat larder. A small room with wire mesh rather than glass in the windows, so that air can circulate to keep the meat cool, the meat larder was often housed in a little building on its own across the manor courtyard. To this day, many Scottish households with regular supplies of their own venison have a larder specially designed for hanging deer carcasses.

The ancient Britons kept domestic cattle, sheep, goats and pigs. Beef was boiled in its own hide, a practice that continued in the Outer Hebrides until the 1720s; the method involved tossing heated stones into a hollow, water-filled log in which the joint to be cooked had been placed. The other major source of meat was forest game, much appreciated by the Normans, whose usual quarry was deer and occasional wild cattle (*Tauri sylvestris*). Meat and brawn from wild boar, which was still hunted for meat until the fifteenth century, were an essential part of Christmas feasting in every manor house. Rabbit and hare, the latter coursed with dogs, were available to the rural poor. The red squirrel, on the other hand, was considered until Tudor times a worthy dish for the aristocracy.

For the medieval table, meat was usually roasted on a spit over the kitchen fire or in the open air – the English loved 'the taste of the fire' – sometimes the joint being parboiled first. Alternatively it could be enclosed in a protective casing of pastry, or the meat was 'frothed' with butter and flour to produce a delicious brown crackling finish. Contemporary cookery books give recipes for the stuffing of poultry, kid and suckling pig. Carving was a very special art that had volumes devoted to its technique, the best-known being Wykan de Worde's *Boke of Kervynge* of 1508.

Foreign travellers visiting eighteenth-century Britain usually commented on the British appetite for their excellent native meat, particularly beef; Per Kalm, the Swedish diplomat, attributed its quality to the sweetness of the English meadow. By now the roasting spit was sometimes mounted on a jack operated by a dog-powered system of wheels and pulleys. There are some fine recipes from this period, ranging from mutton stuffed with oysters to a magnificent Yorkshire Christmas pie that contains a variety of boned fowl and gamebirds.

Meat that was not roasted on the spit was put into the cooling bread oven after the day's baking, and the manor bakehouse offered the same service on request to the local peasantry and labourers. It was not until the nineteenth century that the manor house cook discovered the convenience of the roasting oven.

From Bold Hall, 18th century

BEEF COLLOPS

Take a rump of beef, cut your collops thin and beat them with a cleaver upon a board. Season them with pepper and salt then take a frying pan and some butter. Fry them very quick. Clear of the fat, put to them some good gravy, a little shallot and juice of lemmon. Then serve them up very hot.

FILLET OF BEEF & TRUFFLES

Take the inside of a sirloin of beef that has hung, lard it, then put a fine forc'd meat in it, then lard it with bacon, tye it over with paper and roast it one hour.

The sauce: Make a good crullie of veal and ham, cut a few truffles in half, a pint of Rhinish. Let this boil an hour, then put the juice of two lemons, send it up hot.

BOLD HALL

The Seat of Henry Bold Hoghton, Esq. Bold Hall, built in 1732, was designed by Giacomo Leoni for Peter Bold of Bold, M.P. for the County of Lancaster. It passed through a succession of families to de Hoghton of Hoghton Tower. It was demolished in 1899.

HODGE PODGE

Take some brisket of beef, a breast or loin of mutton. Cut them into pieces. A knuckle of veal, boil these gently in a pot, taking care to scum it well. Throw in four or six onions whole; a dozn. carrots; some whole pepper; two blades of mace; then take 6 heads of celery, as many leeks, one good head of savoy. Scoop some turnips or cut them in dice. Scald them in boiling water, make some good gravy with beef, veal and ham. Season it to your liking. Put your turnips into a saucepan with the sauce that you must take out of the pot, add some gravy to them, which thicken with a little flour. Let them boil till tender, then put yr meat in a dish or tureen and pour the soup over it as likewise your gravy, carrots and turnips.

There should be two hogs ears boil'd from the first with the meat.

FRICASEE OF VEAL

LADY JANE STANLEY

Roast the lean end of a loin of veal, set it by till it is cold, and then cut it in slices. Set on a sauce or stew pan over a stone with butter. Let the butter melt, put in a pinch of flour, some chives and parsley shread. Move the pan over the stove for a minute or two, then having season'd your veal with salt and pepper, put it into the stew pan and give it two or three turns over the stove, then put in a little broth to moisten it and let it boil a little, then put in the yolks of three or four eggs beaten up in cream. Keep it moving over the fire till it is thick enough. Then serve it up.

TO ROAST A HARE

Take half a pint of cream and grate bread into it, a little winter savory, thyme & parsley shread very fine, half a nutmeg grated & half of the hare liver shred but both the white & yolk of an egg & mix all well together (if the stuffing be too light add half a spoonful of flour), then put it into the hare belly & sew it up. Have a quart of cream to baste it with. When the hare is roasted take some of the thickest of the cream out of the dripping pan & make it fine & smooth with a spoon. Have ready drawn a little thick butter & mix it with the cream with a little of the stuffing out of the hare, as much as will make the sauce thick & pour over the hare.

NB. If the whole quantity of cream cannot be had, half cream and half good milk will do, tho it does not answer as well as the whole being cream.

TO MINCE BEEF

Take the lean of beef and mince it a little, larger when you do veal, season it with some chicory and salt. Put it into a tosing pan with a little onion, some good gravey and a glass of red port. Let it stew gently, take out the onion before you dish it and thicken it if you do not find it thick enough.

TO COLLER A BREAST OF VEAL

Take out all the bones lay it in the milk and water, a handfull of salt four hours, then wash it well and wipe it well with a cloth, then season it with mace, nutmeg, cloves, white pepper, a little salt and some anchovies, throw on some sweet margrom, lemmon, thyme and parsley, all chopped fine, the yolkes of two hard eggs cut in slices and lay'd about it. Rowl it tight up and let it boil 3 houres and a half in vinegar, salt and water. You must keep it in this pickle.

TO BARBAQUE A PIG

Kill your pig over night, clean it as for roasting. Cut it open and rub all the inside over with half a quarter of an ounce of red pepper and some salt to your taste. Lay it open on a flat earthen pan or dish with the skin downwarde and let it lie till you purpose dressing it for dinner. See that your oven is very hot, but not to burn. An hour or an hour and a half will bake it sufficiently according to size. If it is not as brown as you chuse it, you may broil it a little which makes it crisper and better. The sauce is the gravey that comes from the pig. Take the fat clean off and put to the gravey as much Madeira wine as suits the palate.

TO DRESS A CALFS HEAD LIKE A TURTLE

Take a calfs head with the skin on and dress it as you do calves feet. Boyle it as you would do for a calves head hash, then cut it into pieces about the breadth of four fingers. Season with ½ an ounce of nutmeg and the same quantity of mace and half a quarter of an ounce of gomekeckery, large spoonfull of salt, a pint of Madeira wine & as much gravey as you think proper made of veal or mutton neak, it requires two hours baking in as hot an oven as for a dinner pye. When its half baked, taste if it wants any more seasoning or thickening, if it do you may thicken it as other gravey then put in your balls maid of a loyne of veal taking the fat instead of suit, and season that with sweet marjaram & parsley, and the same seasoning as before.

If you make a calapee★, you must bone a good large cock & stuff it with the same force meat & bake it as the other. Thers no ocasion for both calapee & balls. If you are dressing fowles, the hearts and soles of them will be a great addition and the throttle of

★Turtle meat.

---

a calves pluck cut in small pieces about the breadth of your thumb. There must be an egg put into your force meat and your dish garnished with yolkes of eggs boyld hard & lemmon.

TO JUGG A HARE

Take your hare, wipe it well but don't wash it, then cut it in pieces but not too small. Put it into a narrow mouthed pitcher with half of half a pint of water and a large glass of port wine, a small bunch of sweet herbes, one large onion stuck with either 2 or 3 cloves, one blade of mace, some whole pepper and a little salt and near half a pound of butter. Set the jugg in a large pot or pan filled with water over the fire, if an old hare it may be set on over night, if a young one early in the morning will do. The fire must be slow. The pitcher tied close over the top with paper. When done enough strain the liquor, scum off the fat and thicken it in a stew pan with a little flowered butter. Let the meat and gravy stew gently over a slow fire for a quarter of an hour.

NB. If the hare is intended for a top dish you may if you please serve to table with small onions blanched and bites of a flitch of bacon either fryd or broiled.

A MUTTON HODGE PODGE

Cut a neck or loyne of mutton into stakes & cut of all the fat. Put it into a degester or pitcher close stop't with lettice, turnups, carrats, cucumbers cut in quarters, sellery & four or five onnians. Put no water to it. Set the degester in a pan of boiling water, and keep the pan fill'd up with water but not so full as to get into the degester. Four hours will stew it.

NB. A hare stew'd in the same way is very good.

TO STEW A RUMP OF BEEF

Take a rump of beef when powder'd about a week & stuff well with all sorts of sweet herbes, pepper salt, a little lemon peel, 2 or 3 anchovies. Shred all very fine, put some lumps of marrow or beef suet, oysters chopt & a little grated bread to make it up into ball & stuff your beef raw & sew it up in a coarse cloth, lay bones across the bottom of the pot & lay your beef on the right side down & let it be just covere'd over with water.

You may put in 2 or 3 onians into the water if you please. Paist up the pot lid very close about that no steam can get out. 5 hours will stew a good handsome rump if you keep it stewing all the while. Make gravey sauce thickned & put in a good many oysters & let them be boyled to take of the rawness. Add 6 yolkes of eggs boyl'd very hard and put whole into the dish by way of garnish. You may put in a little garlick or shalots into the stuffing if you please.

BEEF ALAMODE

Take course pieces of beef well larded with fat bacon, put them into a stewpan with as much water as will just cover them, put in at first – Jamaica pepper, whole large onion in quarters and when the beef is half done some champignern mushrooms, a very little garlick, two or three bay leaves and a little tyme ty'd up together. Just before it's ready to serve up, put in some green parsley, groseley chop'd. If you have a large quantity of meat it will take 7 hours stewing and must be turned when about half done, a less quantity will not require so much time, ('tho it can hardly be done too much) and it is not necessary to turn it. The pan must be covered exceeding close and a weight put on the lid and set over a low fire. If you use it the day it is stewd, the fat should be skim'd off while it is doing. The meat is better for hanging up a day or two before 'tis dressed.

From Sandbeck, 19th century

Copied from Lady Jane Shipton's receipt book.

BEEFSCHEEK PIE

Stew a beef cheek very tender, take out the bones, tie it up in a cloth, put a weight upon it till next day. Then make some forced meat with veal, boil 8 hard eggs, cut the cheek in slices, put at the bottom of the dish, then a layer of the forced meat, another of the eggs, so on till the dish is full. Then put as much of *good* gravy as the dish will hold, put on a puff paste and bake. *Or,* you can make it in a white dish without the crust.

———

DALKEITH SHEEPS HEAD PIE

The day previous to making the pie, get two heads and eight feet, scald them and take off the hair, when this is done, you split them in two and take out the brain and put them in cold water until the next morning:

You then put them in a stewpan of cold water, put them on the fire until they boil, you then immerse them in cold water for a few minutes, take them out, dry them in a cloth and singe them to remove the few hairs that may remain after being scalded. You then put them in a stewpan large enough to hold them, cover them with water, put them on the fire and skim them well when they begin to boil. You then add 2 onions, 2 carrots, a small bunch of parsley, thyme, and bayleaf, 2 cloves and a little salt, let them simmer until they are well done which will require from 7 to 9 hours according to the tenderness of the head. When done remove every particle of bone and spread them on a dish large enough to hold them. Season them well with salt, black pepper and a little Cayenne and put them in a pie dish. In the meantime you strain the liquor through a broth cloth and put it to reduce to a kind of half glaze. When it is reduced enough you pour it over the pie and let it get cold. Then you cover it with puff paste, bake it and let it get cold. To be served cold.

OBSERVATIONS ON THE POT AU FEU

Everyone believes they can make a Boillon Gras but few people really know how to manage a pot au feu, and fewer still have any idea of the importance of what they are doing. It is more a chemical process in fact really. The broth should be made in an earthenware or copper vessel never in one of iron or cast iron as these two metals always give a nasty taste to the broth and discolour it. One quart of water to half a lb of meat is the general measure but more or less can be used according to the quality and quantity of the broth; remains of poultry and cooked or raw meat may also be added but little or no mutton. A small juice of liver also helps to clarify the broth, while a knuckle of veal only weakens and whitens it.

Bouillon pot au feu: Put in the meat and water both at the same time. Place the pot of saucepan on a stove or half hot plate, or on the hob, so that it heats itself gradually, and as fast as the froth rises to the surface skim it off lightly. Add from time to time a drop of water untill the broth ceases to froth and becomes quite clear. Then is the moment to salt and season it. Salt the broth according to taste; the seasoning should be composed of two lb of beef, one large onion larded with 3 cloves, one large carrot cut in two, a parsnip, a turnip, a small head of garlic and 3 leeks tied together, also a stalk of celery when in season.

A larger quantity of vegetable only weakens the soup. When being now seasoned put the lid on sideways so as to allow the steam to escape and let the soup cook gently on the fire for 4 hours. When you want to serve up take out the beef quietly so as not to disturb the soup and then strain. That which remains should be just in a cool place and not covered till quite cold. Some burnt sugar can always be added if the soup requires colouring.

CONSOMME DE GIBIER

¼ lb cooked breast of pheasant, grouse, or partridge
giblets of game
carcase etc.
3 lb knuckle of veal
½ lb ham or bacon
1 large onion
2 turnips
2 carrots
1 bouquet garni
1 small head of celery
3 cloves
1 blade mace
12 peppercorns
1 oz butter
handful cooked green peas
salt, pinch of castor sugar

Remove the flesh from the bird, take off the skin, and cut in small even size dice. Put the bones of game and poultry and the giblets, previously washed, in a stockpot lined with the bacon or ham cut in slices, add a carrot, a turnip and the onion, all cut into slices, the cloves, peppercorns, mace & bouquet garni. Broil over a quick fire for about 15 minutes (if found too dry add 1 oz butter). Cut up the veal, put it with the above & broil a little longer, so as to let it take colour; stir all the time to prevent it from burning.

Moisten with 6 quarts of water, let it come to a boil, take off the scum as it rises to the surface and simmer gently for about 4 hours. Wash the remaining carrot, turnip, celery, scrape & peel, scoop out as many rounds as possible & cook them separately in salted water. They must be firm and yet tender. Put the trimming with the vegetables in the stock & clarify in the usual manner. Strain the cooked vegetable shapes & add them together with the peas to the clarified soup. Simmer for a few minutes. Put the dice of game in a soup tureen, pour the soup over it & serve.

LOCHINCH CASTLE, STRANRAER: MIGNONS D'AGNEAU CHARRON

Cut some rounds from a loin of lamb.

Tie a string around each piece.

Braize for 2½ hours and serve each round on a stuffed tomato.

The sauce in a boat.

Sauce: Make a thick brown sauce and mix in with *mint* sauce which must be made with *lemon* instead of vinegar.

The sauce must not be allowed to boil (or it will curdle) but should be put in a bain marie for about 10 minutes.

The feathered game and poultry larder

The domestic fowl, a descendant of the Indian jungle fowl, was brought to Celtic Britain via Persia, Greece and Gaul sometime before the arrival of the Romans. Greylag and barnacle geese and wild mallard joined the domesticated birds on the menu at about the same time. When the Romans colonized the country, they noted that the ancient Britons did not eat the flesh of their tame birds, although they did eat the eggs, usually roasted in the ashes of the cooking fire.

Wild birds formed an important part of the early British diet, including seabirds such as cormorant, gannet, great auk and gulls. Swan, heron and crane, together with grebe and bittern, remained popular until very recent times. (Wind-dried gannet and cormorant can still be found on Hebridean menus today.) Methods of capture ranged from snares and nets to Roman-inspired birdlime and hawking, originally a Middle Eastern speciality.

The medieval table was laden with delicacies such as stork and bustard, the royal swan and all manner of smaller birds, among them blackbirds, larks, egrets, lapwings and an array of ducks, geese and seabirds. The manor's domestic fowl were penned in a yard so that their eggs could be easily collected by the dairy maid. All medieval manors had a dovecot for the rearing of young pigeons (squabs) for the pot.

Spit-roasting was the usual method of cooking in medieval times, and for little birds there would be small bird-spits. A medieval goose might be stuffed with herbs, fruit and garlic. Wykan de Worde gives exact instructions for the correct sauces in his *Boke of Kervynge:* chawdron sauce for a swan; vinegar, pounded almond and ginger sauce for a boiled fowl; black sauce made from blood pudding to be taken with roasted chicken or duck; a camelyn (cinnamon) sauce for the larger birds such as bittern, crane and heron. Small birds needed only salt and a sprinkling of powdered ginger. Peacocks were left unplucked, skinned then roasted and re-dressed in their magnificent plumage to be presented at banquets with their tails fully displayed. The swan was not dished in its feathers, but roasted and served with a 'pudding de swan neck' – its own elegant neck boned and stuffed. Gamebirds were sometimes stewed with dried fruit and ginger, and hard-boiled egg yolks appear frequently in recipes for stuffings and sauces.

By the nineteenth century, the turkey was the nation's feast dish, replacing swan and peacock at banquets. Flocks of geese and turkeys, driven from as far as Lincolnshire to the markets of London, were a common sight on the roads. The journey took around three months – just the right amount of time from harvest to the Christmas shopping season.

From Bold Hall, 18th century

TO FEED YOUNG TURKEYS

MRS STANLEY

Chop lettuces and dock leaves small while the turkeys are very young, you must chop the greens very small. Put to it some butter, milk and mix it up together like a pudding & feed your young turkeys They will pick it up very fast and need no other food, and be sure keep the little turkeys from the wet, even from wetting themselves with the buttermilk.

PARTRIDGE SOUP

Take a brace of old partridge, skin them and cut them into pieces. Fry them in butter with sliced onions and a little lean bacon, (having first floured them) till they are very brown. Then put a little water into the pan to them, then put them into a large saucepan with four quarts of water in all. Cover it up close and let it stand four hours. Have cellery ready to put into it.

NB. I find by experience that there should be more partridges or less water to make the soup good. If partridges are scarce chicken will do.

A PERIGORD PARTRIDGE PYE

Ld. DERBY

Make a standing pye of good crisp crust. Season your partridges as for other sort of pyes, lay large lumps of forc'd meat between every bird and round the side of your pye, but put none in the belly's of your birds. When bak'd take off the lid, skim off the fat and fill up the pye with strong meat jelly. When cold lay on the lid. You may make a goose pye the same way, only bone the goose and put a fowl bon'd in the inside of it. Make the forc'd meat of the flesh of a rabbit with some slices of ham and some good fresh hogs lard. Mince and then beat it in a mortar, add seasoning of basalick, sarrielda, eschalot and parsley of each a little and the following spices: viz. cloves, black pepper, long pepper & mace, all well pounded. The quantity must be left to the taste of the cooke.

NB. Sarrielda is an annual very like thyme.

PARTRIDGE SAUCE

To a pint of water put half a large onion and half a meatspoonful of peppercorns. Boil all these together till black.
Strain this and put to the liquor grater'd bread, a sufficient quantity to thicken it enough. Three spoonfuls of cream, a lump of butter about the size of a small egg, and boil them.

TO POT WOODCOCKS, MUCH APPROVED

Pick your woodcocks and draw them very clean. To 6 woodcock take an ounce of pepper and as much salt as will answer to make it seasoning and mix and divide it in half. Then work one half into a pound of butter and fill the bodies of the woodcock with it and season ye outside with the rest. Lay 2 pound of butter in the bottom of your pot, then lay the birds with their breasts downwards and cover them with 2 pound of butter. Cover the pot with paste and bake them tender. When they are a little cool take them out of the gravy and let them drain. Then lay them into the pot with the breasts upwards and pour butter over them till the pot is full, the same they were baked in taken clean from the gravy. Let the birds be quite cold before you pour ye butter over them. If the butter they were baked in is grown too cold to pour over them, make it warm over the fire and so pour it on. You may pot partridge, moorgame and snipes in the same way.

TO STUFF A BOIL'D TURKEY

Boil a sweet breast of veal. Chop it fine with a little lemon peel, a handfull of bread crumbs, a little beef suet, part of the liver, a spoonfull or two of cream with pepper and salt, nutmeg and two eggs. Mix all together and stuff your turkey with part of the stuffing. The rest may be boiled or fri'd to lay round it. Dredge it with a little flour, tie it up in a cloth and boil it with milk and water if the turkey is young an hour and a quarter will do it.

CHESNUT STUFFING FOR A TURKEY

Boil the chesnuts and peel them and bruise them fine with a spoon. Mix them up with marrow, pepper and salt and a very little anchovy and an egg to bind it.

From Sandbeck, 19th century

FUMET DE GIBIER

This is made by putting the bones of two grouse or any kind of game into a stewpan with sufficient stock to cover them. Let them simmer gently till the stock becomes reduced to nearly a glaze. Strain through a cloth or fine strainer. Break four yolks of egg into a basin. Add the glaze. Whisk well, season with pepper and salt. Steam in custard cups till the custard is set & serve.

CHICKEN CURRY

Take a good chicken, skin and cut it into joints. Then put 4 oz fresh butter, 3 oz onions, sliced into a stewpan and boil until it becomes a whitish pulp. Then put them into the meat and strew over it a tablespoonful of curry powder and a little arrowroot or soft vegetable such as Jerusalem Artichoke or grated cauliflower tops. A very little will do, let it stew for two hours turning and shaking up the meat all the while until quite tender and falling from the bones. Then take some of the juice of the sour tamarinds, add to it enough to give it an acid flavour. Lemon juice or apple will do if there are no tamarinds. Let it stew half an hour more and then before dishing up put into it a cup of cream. If a dry curry is wanted, take off the lid and allow the meat to absorb the juice and the steam to evaporate. If a wet curry then add some stock of veal or chicken and keep the lid on.

The fish larder

The fish larder was constructed along the same lines as the meat larder.

Fish-eating in Britain has long been linked to religion. When the Saxons began to be converted to Christianity during the sixth century, the missionaries introduced the practice of eating fish on fast days – Fridays and throughout Lent. The demand for 'fasting fish' grew and stimulated fishermen to improve their techniques, and to use salt to preserve their catches for market. The Venerable Bede, high in his tower in the eighth century, mentions eel and salmon fisheries. Whales, porpoises (the venison of the sea and much prized) and sturgeon were all decreed royal fish. When Archbishop Nevill was enthroned at York in 1467, seals featured on the menu for the celebration banquet. Herrings were first 'kippered', or preserved by smoking, in the fifteenth century.

Tudor manor houses used their millponds as storage pools and the larger households employed a fisherman to catch the farmed freshwater fish. Rents were sometimes paid in eel pies. Freshly salted fish was known as 'green fish' and was served with a green sauce. The Elizabethans greatly enjoyed their oysters, there are contemporary recipes for very pretty fish salads decorated with primroses and periwinkles, and potted fish, particularly Severn lampreys, were popular at banquets. Seventeenth-century cooks favoured bisques and stews not unlike modern fish soups. Pike, eel and sturgeon were served stuffed and roasted, with a seasoning sauce of oranges, lemons or gooseberries.

During Cromwell's Commonwealth, fast days were abolished as 'popish', and the English never really re-adopted them. Fishing boats were equipped with tanks for preserving the catch alive, but the more sophisticated Dutch well-vessels replaced them in the eighteenth century: the 'well' occupied the entire middle section of the ship and its walls were pierced to allow seawater to circulate. The freshness of fish brought to market was carefully monitored and strict laws governed the trade – it was believed that disease was transmitted by smell, and the stench of putrid fish was unmistakable. During this century, the manor fishponds were converted into ornamental lakes, although fish for the table was still travelling slowly overland without the protection of refrigeration. By the end of the century, salmon was transported packed in ice. Ice-houses to conserve fish were built both at the catch's landing-point and its ultimate destination in private houses.

The Victorians had a taste for all kinds of salted and smoked fish, particularly for breakfast. There was haddock from Aberdeen, haddock dried and smoked over seaweed fires on the shore by the fishwives of Findon ('finnan haddie'), salmon pickled in beer and salt at Newcastle, and salted and dried salmon from Scotland. The building of the railways during the nineteenth century opened up the south to the northern fishing fleets and trade increased apace.

From Bold Hall, 18th century

TO ROAST STURGEON THE KNOWSLEY WAY

Take a round of fresh sturgeon, pull off ye scales & armour, but leave the skin on. Then make a forcemeat with oysters, anchovies, some parsley & a little Spanish thyme & mushrooms & shallot, minced small. Season with pepper & salt & a little horseradish, grated. Work it up with crumbs of bread & the yolks of eggs & force it through as you do a fillet of veal. Roast it and baste with butter. Thyme, parsley & onions make a sauce with oysters, thick butter, spice, horseradish, a few mushrooms, anchovies & a little lemon peel. Draw it up thick, dish your fish & send it up.

TO STEW LAMPREY OR EEL THE WORCESTER WAY

Skin your fish, season it with a little salt and pepper, nutmeg, cloves and mace not pounded too small, some lemon peel shred small. Put some of this mixture into the belly of the fish and rub it all over well with it. Then cut some thin slices of butter into the bottom of the stew pan. Let the fish be wound round and a skewer thrust through it to turn it within the liquor. Then put it in the stewpan and with it half a pint of gravey, half that quantity of white wine and the same of red with a bunch of sweet herbes, as thyme, winter savoury and hot marjoram, of each very little and one onion sliced. Set it over a slow fire and turn the fish often in the liquor. When it is tender enough put in the anchovies and thicken the sauce with the yolk of an egg stirring in with a little more butter. Serve it up with the liquor it is stewed in for sauce.

TO MAKE A STURGEON PYE

Cut fresh sturgeon in square pieces about an inch thick. Season them with a little salt, pepper and lemon peel minced small. Lay a row in the bottom of your dish or pye pan then a row of shrimps, oysters or cockles seasoned in the same manner till your pye is full. Make force meat of the sturgeon and any other shell fish with pepper, salt and lemon peel, a very little parsley, some onion or shallot chopped very fine and crumbs of bread. Lay a row round the meats, cover all with some butter and if there wants, liquor. Have some ready against it comes out of the oven made of the above mentioned shellfish butter and anchovies and seasoned as above. Before you lay on the butter add some hard eggs cut in halves. Flounder or ray make good forced meats for this dish.

TO DRESS RED HERRING

Put them in cold soft water for 5 or 6 hours, then in boiling water & let them boil 6 minutes, then split and warm them upon a gridiron or before the fire.

If you use them for a pease soup take the skin off.

TO STEW CARP OR TENCH A LA ROYALE

Wash the fish well, gut them and lay them in a marinade of claret or port, some salt and water, three spoonfuls of vinegar, whole spice, mace, cloves and pepper, whole onion and a little lemon peel and horse radish scraped thin. Set them astewing gently for three quarters of an hour and then beat up some butter in a saucepan with some of the fish broth, a couple of anchovies and shrimps. Dish up your fish and pour on the sauce. Garnish with the milt sliced and broiled and the roe sliced and fried.

OYSTER SAUSAGES

Take a pound of the inside of a loyn of mutton, a ½ lb of fresh beef suet – when picked from the skin, a pint of oysters fresh scalded, the beards taken of. Chop them separately very fine and mix them well together, season with pepper, salt and mace to your taste. Add 4 eggs when well minc'd, put into a clean earthen pot, close down, tye it over with a paper. When you use it roul into the shape of sausages adding a few breadcrumbs and a little oyster liquor. Fry them light brown.

From Sandbeck, 19th century

RECIPES FOR COOKING KIPPER

No 1. Cut a piece of kipper about ½ inch thick, butter with fresh butter and put in oven to soak through. Shred the fish with a fork, pepper, return to the oven to make very hot. Eat with toast and butter as a savoury.

No 2. Warm in boiling milk for 3 minutes, pepper and serve very hot in small brown pipkins after pouring off the milk. Eat with very thin toast and butter.

The dry larder

The dry larder, or cook's pantry, is a small room adjoining the kitchen, usually built against an exterior wall so that it has access to a current of fresh air. Today the words *pantry* and *larder* are interchangeable, and both words have their origins in Norman French: *lard* meaning bacon, an important storage item, and *panetrie*, a bread-store. The windows of the Victorian dry larder contained both gauze to keep out insects and glazing so that the windows could be shut in bad weather. The room was used for the storage of cooked meats and prepared dishes. Also stored here is milk, butter, cheese, bread and eggs.

In the medieval kitchen, eggs were staple fare for ordinary days of fasting, although they were not allowed during Lent. Skilled cooks avoided the problem by 'blowing' the eggshells and re-filling them with a thickened white almond milk, with centres made from the same mixture coloured yellow with saffron. The Normans introduced custards and soups thickened with eggs, mixed eggs with wine to make caudles, and appreciated egg and fruit tarts. During the fourteenth century, a mixture called a 'herbolace' – a dish of eggs and herbs much like the modern omelette – became popular. Still more like an omelette was a 'tansy' – an egg mixture fried in butter and flavoured with the eponymous herb. Medieval recipe books contained instructions for the making of both sweet and savoury egg-based fritters, and eggs were also used to enrich bread doughs, although their value as a raising agent was not recognized until the sixteenth century.

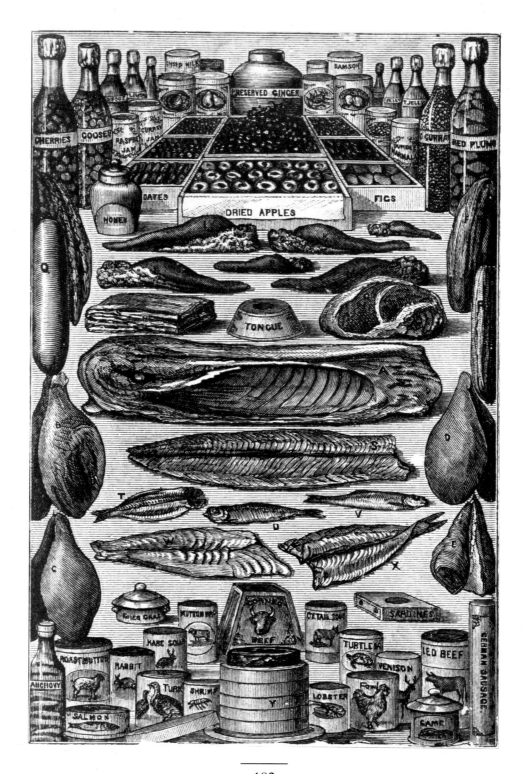

A cookery book of 1596 suggests that four eggs beaten together 'for two hours' be folded into a biscuit mixture. This must have resulted, after considerable effort, in the first sponge cake. Gervase Markham in *The English Hus-wife* of 1615 gives a similar recipe. The English cake was now available, scented with seeds, laced with brandy or containing crystallized fruits, but it remained the province of the skilful cook with plenty of time. Once the trick of transforming egg white into a firm snowy froth had been discovered, many new recipes were invented. They included the spectacular 'dishful of snow', a beautiful confection of beaten egg whites, cream and rosewater, piled up on rosemary branches and sometimes touched with gilt, which formed the *pièce de résistance* at many an Elizabethan banquet. The well-known syllabub was a kind of everyday dish of snow: milk straight from the cow frothed on to a sweetened wine base.

From Bold Hall, 18th century

SOUPE A LA REINE

Take a knuckle of veal about 10 pound, a common fowl, a good slice of lean ham, about six quarts of water. Boil it on a quick fire till the scum rises, skim it quite clean, then add to it two carrots, three turnips, two heads of cellery and two onions. Boil it upon a slow fire till there remains about two quarts, then strain it off and let it stand till it is cold. Skim the fat clean off, then take the breasts of two chickens, 2 oz of sweet almonds, a pint of good cream, the yolks of 5 eggs boil'd hard. Pound the almonds by themselves but put a little cream to them when pounded. Then put all the ingredients together and let them just simmer over a slow fire, then rub it thro' a strainer.

From Sandbeck, 19th century

OEUFS A LA SUISSE

First butter your dish, then sprinkle it with grated Parmesan.
    Break into the dish one egg for each person.
    Season with salt and pepper. Cover the eggs with cream, then sprinkle some more Parmesan on top.
    Bake in a quick oven.

PETIT TIMBALES A LA DUPHINE

Take 2 sweetbreads (cooked) and the equal quantity of ham, and tongue. Cut them into small square pieces with a little chopped mushroom and shalot; pepper and salt to taste. Put altogether into a stewpan with 4 tablespoons of supreme sauce. Then take your Petite Timbale moulds and line them with some good short paste and bake them a very light colour. When done fill them with the sweetbreads and pipe over them some chicken forcemeat. Put them in the oven for 10 minutes when done serve them with a macedoine of vegetables and pour supreme sauce round them.

Serve very hot.

From Bold Hall, 18th century

TO MAKE AN ORANGE PUDDEN

Take half a pound of butter, six ounces of loaf sugar, melt them together over a slow fire, keep stirring all the time, then have ready the yolkes of six eggs well beaten. When the butter and sugar are melted, take it off the fire and stir in the eggs and half a candid orange sliced as thin as possible. Grate in the peel of a Seville orange and juice of a whole orange. Lemon will do as well if no Seville oranges to be had. Only use a less quantity of lemon juice. Beat all together a full half hour. Rowl as thin a paste as possible, and under and over it.

TO MAKE AN ORANGE POSSET

Squeeze the juice of two good Seville oranges and one lemon into a basin that holds about a quart. Sweeten this juice like a syrup with double refined sugar and strain it through a fine sieve. Boil a full pint of thick cream with some orange peel cut thin. When it is pretty cool, pour it into the basin of orange juice through a funnel which must be held as high as you can from the basin. It must stand a day before you eat it.

DUTCH PUDDING

Take 2 pounds of flour; one pound of butter, eight eggs, four spoonful of yest. Then melt the butter in half a pint of milk. Mix them well together and let them stand an hour to rise. Put one pound of currans, clean pick'd & a little loaf sugar. An hour will bake it in a quick oven.

COLLEGE PUDDENS

Take a quarter of a pound of grated bread, a quarter of a pound of currants, a quarter of a pound of suet shredded fine, either lamb, veal or beef will do. Add a very little sugar and a bit of mace or nutmeg make into a paste with the yolks of egg and roll into balls the size and shape of an egg. Fry them in hog lard or beef dripping. Drain them well before the fire from the fat and serve with sugar darted on them. Have sauce made of wine, sugar and butter.

TO MAKE BROWN BREAD PUDDING

MRS A. BOLD

Take half a pound of brown bread grated, half a pound of suet shred fine, half a pound of currants with three eggs beat, a large glass of white wine, a little sugar and nutmeg to your taste. Mix all well together and boil it an hour and a half.

It is good baked.

TO MAKE A PLUMB PUDDING

Take half a pound of beef suet, shred very fine, half a pound of jar raisins ston'd, the crumbs of a penny loaf graterd, two spoonfuls of flour, half a nutmeg, a quarter of a pound of white sugar, 6 eggs well beat, half a jill of cream. Mix all well together and put in a glass of brandy before you put it into the pan. It will take four hours in boiling. It may be put into either the shape of a melon or a cloth.

QUAKING PUDDING

NORTON

Take a pint of cream, 10 eggs, put in the whites of only 3. Beat them very well, mingle them with your cream, 3 spoonfulls of fine flour. Mix it so well that there remain no lumps in it together. Add a little salt and a teaspoonfull of grated ginger. Butter a cloth very well and let it be a thick one. Let it boil for half an hour as fast as you can. Plain melted butter over it.

From Sandbeck, 19th century

MADELIN'S STRAWBERRY SOUFFLE

Serves 6–8

Mix 3 or 4 oz sugar with sufficient strawberry to make a pint of juice. Bruise well. Rub the whole through a tammy cloth, put in a basin in a cold place. Half an hour before the soufflé is wanted whisk and very firm the white of 5 eggs. When ready mix the strawberry purée into the white. Mix lightly and carefully. Put the whole in your soufflé dish prepared as usual. Bake about half an hour or 25 minutes. Serve hot.

This soufflé should be only mixed the last minute before put in the oven or else the strawberry will go to the bottom and it will not be so good.

PUDDING A LA RUSSE

DITTON PARK, SLOUGH

Line a plain Charlotte mould with short paste. Fill with dry rice to prevent the paste puffing up. Bake to a light golden colour. When done, carefully take rice out. Make custard with 6 or 7 yolks of eggs, 1 pint of milk, sugar to taste, flavour with vanilla (very little). Steam in a mould or jar the same size as the pastry lining until quite firm. Then let it get cold, and just before serving, spread a little apricot jam in the bottom of the pastry. Turn the custard into it and turn on to the dish. Pour apricot sauce round and a little whipped cream at each end.

PAIN PERDU

44 CHARLES STREET, BERKELEY SQUARE, W

Cut slices of bread nearly an inch thick and about 3 inches square. Soak them in milk from ½ an hour to an hour according to the freshness of the bread. Dip each slice in the yolk of an egg and then fry in butter till quite brown.

Prepare some caramel sauce. Pour the same over the toast when the latter is very hot and serve immediately.

SOUFFLE RICE PUDDING

Put 3 oz rice, 1 pint of milk and two lumps of sugar into a stewpan. Set it on the stove and let the rice cook gradually and well. When cooked take it off the stove to cool, then stir in the yolks of 2 eggs and whipped whites of 4. Well butter a pie dish and dust over with sugar. Put in the mixture and bake in a moderate oven for half an hour.

From Bold Hall, 18th century

CREAM PANCAKE

A pint of cream, 2½ spoonfulls of flower, 3 eggs leave out one white. Beat these well then add 6 ounces of butter melted and cold. They must be only fried on one side in a copper pan that is tin'd. A quick fire.

TO MAKE LORD CARLISLE'S SACK POSSET

Take one quart of cream and boil in it a little whole cinnamon & two or three flakes of mace. To this proportion of cream put in 9 yolkes of eggs & four of the whites and a pint of sack. Beat your eggs very well and then mingle them with your sack. Put in one quarter of a pound of sugar into the wine & eggs with half a nutmeg grated. Set the bason on the fire with the wine and eggs and let it be hot. Then put in the cream boiling from the fire, pour it on and hold it high up when you pour it on the wine but stir it not. Cover it with a dish & when it is settled serve it up.

The still-room
and store cupboard

The country house still-room was originally the place where cordials and perfumes were distilled. Its first recorded appearance is in the sixteenth-century list of household offices for the Elizabethan mansion, Hengrave Hall. By the mid-Victorian age, the still-room had become a secondary kitchen, kept for the use of the housekeeper and her assistant, the still-room maid. In it were made and stored the household's supplies of preserves, jams, cakes and biscuits, as well as tea and coffee. By then it was also sometimes used for pastry and bread-making.

The most important non-essentials in the country-house store cupboard were spices and sweetening agents, both used extensively in the all-important art of preserving perishable foodstuffs. Spices and herbs have been used in Britain since the earliest times. Bronze Age Britons liked thyme and fennel as flavourings, and coriander seeds have been found on the sites of their settlements. The Romans had a particular liking for pepper, of which they had three varieties. Saffron and mustard they grew themselves, although probably not in Britain. A favourite Roman mustard was mixed with pounded almonds and honey to be eaten with sausages, blood puddings and a form of spiced haggis very like the modern Scots dish. Medieval English merchants bought their spices at the great Continental trading fairs. Pepper, although still expensive, was to be found in every Norman spicebox and most Anglo-Saxon ones as well.

The medieval lady of the manor kept her more costly spices locked up in her store-chest and issued small quantities to the head cook on request. The taste of the time was for strong spice mixtures, not necessarily, as before, to disguise tainted food since supplies to the manor kitchens were by then usually fresh enough. Colour was important too, and indigo, saffron and sandalwood were all favourite colouring agents. The next additions to the spicebox came from the New World: by the seventeenth century, vanilla – the seed pods of an orchid – and capsicum peppers for paprika and cayenne were imported from America; allspice, or Jamaica pepper, arrived from the West Indies.

The Crusaders originally introduced sugar from the canefields round Tripoli to their honey-loving compatriots. From then on sugar, usually refined in its country of origin, was added to the cargoes of the spice ships trading at the Channel ports of England. Extraordinarily elaborate confections in sugar became the centrepieces of banquets, quite as magnificent as the medieval roast peacock, and sugar-sculpting continued to be fashionable throughout the eighteenth and nineteenth centuries. Sugar itself was also increasingly used to sweeten coffee, tea and chocolate.

From Bold Hall, 18th century

FISH SAUCE

Take half a pound of butter, two spoonfuls of good gravy, a handfull of peeled shrimps, four anchovies, a small onion, a piece of horseradish. Dust in a little flour. Let all stand together in your saucepan an hour. Then melt and heat all together, stiring in a small spoonful of catchup. Take out the onion and horseradish when you serve it to table.

A COMPOSITION FOR ALL SAUCE

A pint of claret or white wine
20 pepper corns
A bunch of thyme
A large onion stuffed with a few cloves
6 Anchovys
6 Spoonfuls of Vinegar
A little ginger
A stick of horse radish

All these must be boil'd till the anchovys are dissolved. It will keep corked up in bottles a long time. One spoonful to half a pint of butter will do for fish and a little in any dish is good.

WALLNUT CATCHUP

Take a hundred of wallnuts. They must not be riper than for pickling, then knock them small and strain them. Boil and scum the liquor, then put an oz of nutmeg, half an oz mace, cloves and pepper, one pint of vinegar, 2 spoonfuls of salt. Let it boil till it is as red as claret. When cold bottle it up. Don't use it till six months old. The better the older 'tis kept.

GOOSEBERRY VINEGAR

Six pound of bruised gooseberries to a gallon of water to stand a fortnight in a warm place and to ferment and the fruit to rise up to the top which it will do in about a fortnight. Draw off the liquor and strain it. To every gallon of liquor put a pound of brown sugar which will make it ferment a second time. When done working stop the vessel up close. It will be fit to use in 6 months. But it must still be kept warm.

CUCUMBER VINEGAR

Fifteen large cucumbers pared and cut in thin slices. Put them into a pan with a quart of vinegar, add three or four onions sliced, a few shallots, a little garlick, some salt, ground peper, and a little Cayenne pepper. Let them stand 3 or 4 days, then strain it & filter it. Bottle it with some whole pepper.

NB. It must be made with ye sharpest vinegar.

INDIAN PICKLE

Take ginger one pound, lay it a night in salt and water, then scrape it and cut it into thin pieces and put it in a bottle with dry salt. Let it remain their till the rest of your ingredients are ready. Take one pound of garlick, peel and cut it in pieces and salt it for three days. Then wash it and salt it again and let it stand three days longer. Then wash it and lay it on a sieve to dry in the sun.

Take cabbages cut in quarters, salt them for three days then squeeze the water well out of them and set them to dry in the sun.

Sallary and cauliflowers must be done in the same manner but of the sellery you are only to take what is good of the white part. Radishes are done in the same way but they must be scraped and the green young tops left on. French beans and asparagus must be salted only two days and then must have a boil up in salt and water. They are afterwards to be dry'd as the others. Long pepper must be salted and dry'd in the sun but not too much.

Take a stone or glass jarr and put all these ingredients into it with one quart of the very strongest vinegar you can get, three quarts of a weaker sort, mustard seed and a little turmarick, brused very fine. Fill your jarr 3 parts full, look at it a fortnight after and if you see occasion fill it up again.

Apples, plumbs, grapes, carrats, peaches, cucumbers, melons, etc are all done in the same manner. You need never empty the jarr but as the things comes in season, put them in and fill it up with vinegar.

NB. Of the fruit you pickle must be never ripe wallnuts and red cabbage can't be pickled in this manner.

From Sandbeck, 19th century

ANCHOVY BUTTER

4 Anchovies boned
a Bunch of parsley, boiled let it be cold
2 oz of butter pounded together and then rubbed through a hair seive and made into pats.

CURRY POWDER

LORD THYNNE'S RECEIPT

Coriander seeds, 3 oz
Pale tumeric, 6 oz
Black pepper, ¼ oz
Ginger, ¼ oz
Cardomons, ¼ oz
Cummin seeds, ¼ oz
Celery seeds, ½ oz
Fennell seeds, ½ oz
Cayenne pepper, ¼ oz

Pound separately & mix well. To be kept in a baller & cover from the light.

From Bold Hall, 18th century

TO KEEP MUSHROOMS ALL THE YEAR

Take small buttons and wipe them clean with a piece of flannel & fling them into salt and water as you rub them. Then do but give them a boil or two up, and when cold have ready some strong brine that will bear an egg and put the mushrooms into small pots and put the brine to them, into pots that will hold no more than what you will use at once, and cover them close with mutton suet and tye bladders over them. When you use them freshen them in warm water and change the water till you think they are fresh enough. Some boil them quite as much as you would do for pickling before ye brine is put to them & I believe they will keep better. They are very good this way either for fricasees or to put in sauce.

From Sandbeck, 19th century

CUMBERLAND SAUCE

Take a pint of fresh red currants juice
a stewpan
2 tablespoons of golden syrup
2 tablespoons of common vinegar
2 tablespoons of King of Oude Sauce
2 of Worcestershire Sauce
a Stalk of horseradish, grated

Boil all together for 10 minutes then strain through a wire strainer and stand covered to get cold.

If fresh red currants are not in season, a pot of jelly would answer.

From Bold Hall, 18th century

A PEPPER CAKE

Take two pounds of fine flour, three pound and a half of treacle, a ¼ of an ounce of cinimon, a ¼ of an ounce of mace and cloves mixed, half a gill of brandy, an ounce and a half of carraway seeds, ½ an ounce of beaten ginger, two spoonfuls of yeast, ½ a gill of ale and two eggs.

Mix all together very well and add what candid orange and lemon you please. Bake it in a tin. You may add more spice if you please but this quantity is allways thought enough.

CASSIA

Take 1 lb sugar finely sifted, 1 oz & a quarter of Japan earth finely sifted. Mix them with orange flower water and rose water not quite so stiff as for a candy; boil it till it will drop & come clear off. Just before you take it of add 6 grains of amber grease. Mush fine ground with a little sugar in a morter.

RED GINGERBREAD

Take ½ an ounce of cinimon, a ¼ of an ounce of anniseed, a ¼ of an ounce of liquroise powder, ½ an ounce of ginger, three or four cloves. Beat and seive these well, then take a pound of powder sugar, an ounce and half of canders and a gill of claret, six ounces of Jordan almonds blanch'd and beat with rose water. Set all these on the fire to boil, keep stirring all the while then put to it by degrees the crumbs of two white stale penny toasts which have been grated and dried and put through a sive. Let it boil then put it by to dry.

MRS SCRATONS CAKES

Take a quarteron of fine flower and two spoonfulls of oatemeal. Pass thro a sive. Six ounces of butter, melt it in 3 jells of milk, two spoonfulls of yest. When it is about blood warme make it into a paste and let it stand for an hour to rize. Then make it into little thin cakes and bake 'em in a slow oven, and not too *hard*.

NUNS BISKETS

Take the whites of 6 eggs, beat them to a froth, half a pound of almonds, blanch them and beat them with the froth of the whites of your eggs. As it rises take the yolks and a pound of fine sugar, beat these together well, and mix your almonds with the eggs and sugar, then put in a quarter a pound of flour. Bake them in little tins in a quiet oven. Half the quantity in general is enough.

TO MAKE BUNS

Rub half a pound of butter into three pounds of flour & put in half a pound of currants. Mix half a pint of milk and water made warm with 3 or 4 spoonfull of good barme & a little salt. Beat them well together & put it thro a sieve then put it to the flour and make a paist – something lighter than french bread. Work it well & let it stand before the fire to rise well, then work it well again & make into buns letting them stand twenty minutes before they are put into the oven. The oven must not be too hot.

BROWN WAFFERS

Take the yolks of 2 eggs, a pint of milk or cream. Beat your eggs with some of your milk and make it as thick with flour as thin batter. Mix it well and sweeten it as you please. Put in some cinnamon sifted, 2 spoonfulls of sack. Mix it all well together & let it stand for 4 hours & they bake the better.

NB. A large teaspoonfull makes a waffer.

GINGERBREAD CAKES

Take three pound of flour, a pound and a half of treacle and a pound and a half of brown sugar, 3 ounces of ginger beat and season'd, one ounce and a half of carraway and correander seeds pounded, one ounce of mace, two nutmegs, a pound of melted butter, a glass of brandy, five eggs well beaten, three ounces of candid orange.

   Mix all very well together to a paste. Make it into little thin cakes and bake on tin sheet. Keep near a fire that it may be crisp.

The salting-room and smokehouse

Around 500 BC the climate of the British Isles started to grow gradually cooler and wetter. Iron Age Britons, used to preserving food by simple wind-drying methods, began to find this inadequate, and added smoking and salting to the process. In the early days, the techniques lacked sophistication, and the smoking was done over a damped-down open fire. In late medieval times, special recesses in the chimney by the cooking fire (often mistaken for priest-holes) were provided where hams and flitches (salted pork) could be hung to smoke. In Scotland, the fisherman's catch would often be salted immediately on shore or, later, on the boats taking the fish south to market. Smoking might be carried out either in special smokehouses near the shore or, in more primitive fashion, over fires made of dried seaweed. Medieval smoked salmon was a stiff and salty plank of dried fish, almost unrecognizable to the modern gourmet.

Until the seventeenth century, most domestic cattle and sheep were killed off in the autumn as there was no way to feed a great many of them through the winter. Their flesh therefore had to be preserved for as long as possible, and the problems of brining, smoking, potting and conserving were a major preoccupation of the medieval housekeeper. The innovation in Georgian times of turnips for winter fodder, which allowed more of the beasts to be overwintered, took the worst pressure off the cook, although considerable quantities of meat and fish still had to be preserved during times of glut. At the same time, a new source of demand for preserved foods appeared: sailors faced with the long sea voyages of exploration and trade needed as much well-preserved food as possible.

Salt for pickling should be as near its natural raw state as possible. A small amount of salt petre (half an ounce to 100 pounds of meat) must be included in the pickling solution so that the salt will 'take' well and give the meat the pink tinge that appears after cooking. Too much salt petre will turn the pickling solution green and the meat hard.

From Bold Hall, 18th century

TO PICKLE STURGEON

Take your sturgeon and scrape it free from the blood, then rub it well with salt, and let it lie 12 hours and then put it into water for 12 hours more. Then take it out and tieing it up with bafo very tight. Put it in a kettle with either stale ale or beer which is most convenient with a good handfull of whole ginger and the same quantity of white pepper and let it boyle for 1½ hours. Then taking it off the fire and then take out your sturgeon, and letting your liquor stand then it is cold, and then scum off all the fat and oil. Then to about a gallon of your liquor, put in about a pint of vinegar, then putting your sturgeon into the liquor which will keep it as long as you please.

TO PICKLE SALMON LIKE STURGEON

Cut a piece about 9 or 10 inches out of the middle of the salmon, cut up the belly of the piece and take out the chine without cutting it through the back, season it well with black pepper and salt. Let it lye in that seasoning 10 or 12 hours, and then tye it up with bafo in the same manner as sturgeon is done. For the pickle you must boil together two quarts of alegar★, one of water, one ounce of black pepper, ½ an ounce of mace, ½ an ounce of cloves, ½ a handfull of salt and some bay leaves. When it boiles put in the salmon and let it boil threequarters of an hour, then take it out and when the pickles is cold put it in again and keep it close covered. It will keep good near a quarter of a year.

★Sour ale.

TO DRY A GOOSE

Rub the geese well with brown sugar and all the salt mixt well together. After they have laid a fortnight, then hang them up in a warm place, but not too near the fire with white paper covered over them. The paper must hang so as not to touch them and must be open a little at the bottom. Before they are used they should hang in a cellar or damp place for a day or two and then steep them for a day or two in cold water, changing it once or twice, so soften them and plump them up, then boil them and eat them with cabbage boild & put over them. Some like a pease pudding or greens or what sort of greens you please.

TO PICKLE BEEF, PORK & VEAL WHICH WILL KEEP GOOD IN THE HOTTEST CLIMATE

MR WILLIAMS

Take 4 gallons of good water to which add 1½ lb of sugar and 2 oz salt petre, 6 lb of salt. Put the whole into a clean pan & let it boil being careful to take all the scum off as it rises. When it is quite clear, take it off the fire and let it stand untill quite cold, and having put the meat you want to preserve into the vessel you mean to keep it in, pour in the liquor untill the meat is quite cover'd. If you keep your meat a considerable time, it will be necessary once in 2 months to boil the pickle over again, taking off the scum as it rises & adding to it when boiling 2 oz sugar & ½ lb of salt. It will keep 12 months.

MRS BALLS' FOR CURING HAM

Rub them very well with brown sugar and let them lie till next morning. Then to each ham just 2 ounces of salt petre beat very fine. Rub it on with your hand very well at two or three different times. Then let it lie 24 hours, then to each ham put 1 lb bay salt beat very fine. Rub it on 2 or 3 times a day, a little at a time after the salt is done rub your ham with the brine thrice or four times a day with your hand very well.

In winter they may lie three weeks in the pickle but in warm weather a fortnight is long enough. Smoak them a little.

RUM PUNCH LORD BENTICK (1791)

The juice of six lemons, four ounces of loaf sugar, a quart of boiling water.
Strain it through a napkin, then add to it a pint of rum, and a little nutmeg.

TO PICKLE OYSTERS

Take four dozen of oysters. Wash them clean in their own liquor and then strain the liquor through a muslin and put it on the fire. Let it boil up once or twice, scim it well, then put in your oysters with one ounce white pepper and five or six blades mace and a little salt. Let them boil till they begin to shrivel up, then take them out of the liquor and put them into the pot, stop it close and add to the liquor six spoonfuls of vinegar and four of mountain wine. Let it boil a quarter of an hour, then pour it hot on the oysters and keep them from the air.

From Sandbeck, 19th century

PICKLE FOR TONGUES

LOCHINCH CASTLE, STRANRAER

2 gallons of water
4 to 5 pounds salt
½ lb salt petre
½ lb moist sugar

Boil for almost 5 minutes then let it stand until cold. Well wash and rub the tongues with salt before putting them in the pickle.

They will be ready for use in a fortnight.

The dairy

Milk has been a staple ingredient of the British diet since prehistoric days. Storage was always a problem, and early milk drinkers probably drank it soured into curds and whey. The Celts took the process a stage further: they were excellent coopers and made butter in wooden buckets. The making of hard cheese for keeping was the next important development. Soft cheese made of soured curds will not mature – it simply goes bad. True cheese is made by the addition of rennet, a mammal's digestive juice, to new milk.

Butter was the frying oil of the Middle Ages; olive oil, which could not be produced in Britain, was scarce and expensive, and medieval cookery and medical books all instruct the cook to 'boil in butter'. Pies were often sealed in butter, and butter was used as a conserving and air-excluding agent in the potting of meat and fish. Milk and its products were known as 'white meats' and were essentially a peasant food. The Normans particularly liked junket – fresh cream curdled with rennet and then drained of whey into little rush baskets.

The dairy of the medieval manor house processed both cows' and sheep's milk. In some areas of the country, goats provided part of the supply and Cheddar cheese was originally made from goats' milk. The milking of sheep continued into the sixteenth century, when their importance to the wool trade made farmers reluctant to use them for any other purpose. The manor household did not take its milk raw, but the dairy was kept busy making cream, clotted or fresh, and butter, and the skimmed milk could be made into cheese or drunk as buttermilk. Fresh curd cheese was known as green or young cheese. From the seventeenth century onwards, cheese was used in cooking and appears regularly in recipes, mixed into sauces, sprinkled on soup, and used as a topping on savoury dishes of vegetables and meat.

As life became more leisured in Georgian times, the dairy, furnished with chairs, tables and delicate china, was sometimes turned into an extension of the drawing-room where the ladies could retire to take a syllabub or fresh warm milk. A Victorian dairy on the grand scale occupied its own building apart from the main house. If the household was relatively modest, the dairy was likely to be a small room similar to a larder and adjoining the kitchen – although not leading into it because of the kitchen steam. The walls were tiled and the floor was made of stone or tiles with plenty of drainage so that the room could be thoroughly and frequently cleaned.

From Bold Hall, 18th century

YORK CURDS

Take a quart of new milk and a pint of cream; four quarts of water, a very little bit of salt. Set it over a clear stove fire. Then take 8 eggs, leave out four whites, beat them well and strain them through a seive. Mix with them a pint of sour cream and when your pan is just at boiling put in the eggs and sour cream, stir it well to stop it settling to the bottom. As the curd rises keep putting in a little cold water. When they are well risen take them off the fire and let them stand a little to sadden. Then lay a cloth over a very clean sieve and take the curd off with an egg slice and lay it on ye sieve. Make them ye day before you use them.

CREAM CHEESE

MRS BERENS

Take a pint of good cream and 3 pints of new milk. Let it boil till it is ready to boil, then pour it into a large pan and put to it 3 spoonfulls of rennet. Let it stand a full hour and then put it carefully into a straw vat. Turn your cheese (vat and all) for eight days, every day and it will be fit to eat.

A THIN WINTER CHEEZE

MR CHAMBRE

Take all new milk but no cream. Put it together to be tender and when all the whey is off put the curd into cold water for half an hour, then put it into the cheeze vatt but do not break it at all but squeeze it a little and then put it under your press, and when it has been under about half an hour slit it in two or three as you like best. The next morning take them from under the press and salt them a little.

The thin toasting cheeze is made the same way, only adding all the Nights Cream to the new milk. This cheeze may be made the end of Sept or in October.

CHEEZE TO EAT LIKE CREAM CHEEZE AS SOON AS MADE

Shave a pound and half of the mildest cheeze you can get, pound it in a marble mortar with half a pound of fresh butter and a small glass of white wine till it is perfectly incorporated. Put it close down in a shallow pot and cut it out as you use it. The milder the cheeze the more like cream.

The brewhouse and cellar

The earliest alcoholic drink known to have been drunk in Britain was almost certainly mead. A mixture of honey and water left to stand will quickly ferment, and there is plenty of evidence to suggest that pre-farming, hunter-gatherer Britons enjoyed a beakerful. The Romans planted vineyards, but inevitably wine produced in Britain lacked the fullness and sweetness so much prized by the Romans. Their solution was to mix in *'defrutem'*, a concentrated must of sweet grape juice that they imported from their southern vineyards. Trade in wine dropped off after the departure of the Romans, and it was only the monasteries which kept the tradition of winemaking alive, although sweet wines from as far as Crete were imported and appreciated.

The Anglo-Saxons set up ale-houses in the villages and at crossroads for the refreshment of travellers; the great British pub has its origins in these taverns. Medieval manor brewhouses turned out large quantities of ale, cider, metheglin and mead, and in the fourteenth century, a new beer from Flanders, its flavour bitter with hops but having a much longer life, began to gain in popularity. According to William Harrison, lord of his own manor and a sixteenth-century chronicler, the house brewing was 'practised by my wife and hir maid servantes'. This brewing was, he tells us, 'once a moneth' and produced 200 gallons for regular household consumption. In affluent households, ale was consumed a year after it was made, at full strength just before it went sour.

The cellars of seventeenth-century country houses were stocked with brandy from France, particularly from the district of Cognac and the new distilleries of Martell and Hennessy; genever imported from Holland; and perhaps some rumbullion or kill-devil from the West Indies. The liquor was stored in wooden casks, and when it was needed for the table, the wine was decanted straight into bottles equipped with wooden bungs. Cork stoppers were introduced towards the end of the century, and made it possible to mature particularly good wine in bottles. The English taste for port grew, and this fortified wine was drunk in country houses in enormous quantities: three- and four-bottle-a-day men were not uncommon in leisurely pre-Victorian days.

From Bold Hall, 18th century

GINGER WINE

12 lb of sugar to 10 gallons of water, & whilst cold the whites of 6 eggs, well beat. Stir them all well together when near boiling, skim it well, take half a pound of the very best ginger, just bruise it & put it to the liquor when boiling, boil it twenty minutes. Pare very thin the rinds of 10 lemons, pour the liquor boiling hot upon them. When quite cold put it into a cask with two spoonfuls of good yeast. Take off the whites of the lemons, when pared, cut them into slices, taking out the seeds, put them into the liquor with half an ounce of isinglass. Close it up the next day, without stirring.

It will be ready to bottle in a fortnight. Put a raisin in each bottle.

DIRECTIONS FOR BREWING YE ESSENCES INTO BEER

For a cask of thirty gallons take ten oz of ye essence and 20 lb molasses or treacle. Mix both well together in about 5 or 6 gallons of warm or cold water according to ye climate. After ye liquor has been well stirred together till it bears a froth pour it into ye cask, which fill up with water. Add then for ye first time one pint of good yest or grounds of porter (afterwards ye grounds of ye same beer will always serve for ye next brewery); shake ye cask well, and set it by for 2 days to work. After which let it be bunged up and in a few days it will be fit to draw off into bottles which ought to be well corked and set by for a week or 10 days in a cool cellar.

Then it will turn out as fine dark Spruce beer as ever was drunk.

NB. The essence is warranted to keep in all climates for years if close covered from ye air. Three tablespoonfuls of it is equal to 4 oz by weight. Sold by Thomas Bridge, at No 21 Bread Street, London at 9d. ye pod of 20 oz which will make 63 gallons.

From Sandbeck, 19th century

RUM OR BRANDY SHRUB

To every gallon of spirit put a quart of the juice of orange & a pound & quarter of fine loaf sugar. Stir them all together til ye sugar is disolved, then put in a pint of new milk boiling hot, stir it a little & let it stand till next day, then run it through a jelly bag till fine. Bottle it. To every 3 dozen of oranges put 6 lemons.

To make almond shrub: Add a quarter of a pound of bitter almonds blanched and pounded, mixed with one pound of water.

GINGER WINE

5 gallons of water
4 pounds of lump sugar
two ounces of ginger sliced thin

Boil it an hour, skimming it well. Empty it into a tub, let it stand till cold. Then put it into a vessel with the very thin peels and the strained juice of 5 lemons and one pint of Brandy. Put half a spoonful of yeast on the top and stop it down close. In a fortnight it will be fit to bottle, in a fortnight more to drink.

FOR THREE HOGSHEADS OF SMALL BEER

9 Bushell of Malt
1 Bl. Wheat and 1 Bl. Oats malted together
1 pound of hops

Boil them 2 hours and half. Work it 2 days.

From Bold Hall, 18th century

THE DUKE OF NORFOLKS PUNCH

To every gallon of brandy put 6 lemons & 6 oranges. Pare them thin & put them in the brandy. Let them stand 24 hours, then take 6 quarts of water, 3 pounds of loaf sugar. Boil it half an hour and clear it with the whites of 4 eggs, then strain out the peel from the brandy & squeeze the juice of the lemons & oranges into it through a strainer. Then mix altogether & run it in a vessel. Let it stand six weeks then bottle it & it will keep years.

TO MAKE SHRUB

Take a quart of orange juice, put 3 quarts of brandy or rum & one pound and half of loaf sugar. Put it into a vessel with room for it to shake, cork it up close & shake it well for 8 or 10 days. Let it stand till it is fine then bottle it. It is generally fine in a fortnight, if it is not fine let it stand longer.

A FRENCH LIQUEUR

To one bottle of brandy put 3 china oranges, whole, half a pound of loaf sugar and 3 cloves.

Let it infuse 6 weeks near the fire. Then philtre it through paper into a bottle.

It has been found necessary to put near another bottle of brandy to it afterwards.

GREEN GOOSEBERRY WINE

Gather your berries at the full growth, just crack them. To every 3 quarts of fruit put a quart of spring water, let them stand cover'd in a cool place 24 hours, then draw it off through a large hair sieve. Take what runs very clear and to every gallon of liquor put 3 lbs of loaf sugar, stir it well till the sugar be disolv'd, cover it and let it stand 24 hours. Scum and tun it, stir it in the vessel, bung it close and set it in the seller. After 16 hours may clay it up & not open it till next March in a calm season except it works much in the barrel, in that case, you may draw the vent peg a little. Put to 10 gallons when you tun it 6 pennyworth of isinglass cut very small lose in the barrel. Draw it off for bottling very slowly. Put no sugar in the bottles. A 10 gallon cash requires 102 quarts of fruit, 8 gallons and 2 quarts of liquor, 30 lb of sugar.

RAISIN WINE

8 pounds of best Malaga raisins well clear'd from the stalks. To one gallon of water, in this proportion, fill your cask about three quarters full or better, the liquor should be stirr'd every day for 3 weeks or a month or till the fermentation goes off, and then fill'd up with more liquor which you should have ready in another cask. When it has done working put in some brandy, and bung it up. It should remain in the cask 12 months or longer before it is bottled. 2 quarts of brandy is sufficient for a pipe.

From Sandbeck, 19th century

BARLEY WATER

fr. a Practical Lady – Morning Post

Six lemons
¼ lb pearl barley
¼ lb loaf sugar

Peel the rind off the lemons very thin without any of the white part. Then put the rind on to the fire in a little stewpan with enough water to cover. When boiled a few minutes about 5 pour it all in a jug large enough to hold three quarts of water. Then wash the barley very clean and put on the stove till it boils, then strain off the hot water from the barley and wash it well again. Strain it off and put it in the jug with the lemon rind, then get the 6 lemons and peel off all the white part and cut each one in three slices and put in the same jug. Get your sugar and put on the fire in a little stewpan with some water till it boils, then pour it in with the other ingredients. Get three quarts of boiling water ready pour in the jug. Leave it in a cool place till cold and strain it before serving.

The country house garden

The medieval manor garden – a large, square, walled enclosure sited alongside the orchard – laid the foundations for the modern country house garden. It was carefully manicured, with arbours, paths and grassy seats. The flower strains were still very close to the indigenous wild species, and the garden had few vegetables – although fruit trees had been planted since Roman times. Marigolds, violets and columbine were grown to flavour soups; parsley, mint, violets, rose petals, primrose buds, daisies and dandelions were used in salads. Cabbages and leeks were the favoured green vegetables. Cultivated root vegetables included parsnips, turnips, radishes and carrots. Wild strawberry plants were transplanted from the woods, and early Tudor gardeners added rhubarb, lettuces, apricots, lemons, pippins and artichokes.

Elizabethan gardens reflected the flamboyant Tudor tastes. For the first time, they were architect-designed with statuary, yew hedges and fountains, terraces and steps, formal flowerbeds, and a maze to amuse the ladies. Melons, cucumbers and the 'knobbie rootes' of the newly arrived potato were added to the kitchen garden. Tender fruit trees were moved into the shelter of the walled garden: 'apricockes', peaches and nectarines ripened against south-facing walls, while quinces and plum trees were pinned against the west wall. Soft fruit such as gooseberries, currants and raspberries grew alongside the root vegetables and herbs. Flowers and sweet herbs were dried and used in jars of pot-pourri to scent Elizabethan rooms. Traditionally each room had a particular predominating fragrance: damask rose in the drawing-room, walnut or bay leaves in the library, verbena and lemon balm in the bedrooms, lavender in the linen closet.

By the Georgian era, gardens had become less formal. Under the influence of landscape gardeners such as Lancelot 'Capability' Brown, woods and sloping lawns replaced the topiary, and the vegetation was allowed to grow naturally and romantically luxuriant. Dedicated gardeners began to grow more exotic fruits and vegetables; melons, tomatoes, figs and grapes were forced under glass, and in 1560 Sir Francis Carew managed to grow oranges and lemons. Even pineapples were reared with some success, although the pineries were abandoned when better fruit began to arrive by sea from the West Indies.

The Victorian garden reflected Victorian virtues: everything had its proper place. Produce from the kitchen garden played an important part in the family's diet, providing all the vegetables and fruit needed for home consumption. Plain boiled vegetables were considered wholesome family fare, and fruit was a required part of the dessert course for the adults. Purpose-built greenhouses produced flowers and pot plants for the 'big house' throughout the year. Delphiniums and Chinese lanterns were planted to be dried for winter flower vases. The mint patch was cultivated for mint sauce, the parsley patch for parsley sauce.

From Bold Hall, 18th century

ONION SOUP

Put about half a pound of butter into a saucepan, let it brown a little. Then put in six large onions cut pretty small, which fry till brown, dust into them a little flour, add to these small mutton or beef broth with a little salt and pepper and a little grated nutmeg. Boil a small french loaf or role a quarter of an hour in it, then heat up the yolks of six eggs with a little broth and when off the fire add these, but don't let it boil after the eggs are put in.

GREEN PEASE SOUP

Take five or six cucumbers and pare and slice them, take the white part of as many cos latuces, a sprig of mint, two or three onions, a little pepper and salt, a pint of young pease, a quarter of a pound of butter. Put these together into a stew pan and let them stew in their own liquor for an hour and half (or till they are tender). Then boil two quarts of old pease, sift them thro a sieve, then put them with the ingredients that have been ster'd into two quarts or more (as you like for thickness) of the water the old pease were boil'd in. You must add a quarter of a pound of butter, then just let it boil up. Then put it into your tureen.

TURNIP SOUP

Take four large turnips, cut them in quarters, put them into a stewpan with a quarter of a pd. of butter. Let them stew till they are quite soft, then put to them the broth of a knuckle of veal boil'd in 4 quarts of water, reduce it to 2 quarts, add to it a little mace, white pepper, onions, carrots, a few sweet herbs with the crumbs of a penny loaf. Then strain all through a seive and whiten with a gill of good cream.

TO STEW CUCUMBER

Pare a dozen cucumbers and slice them thick. Put them to drain then lay them on a cloth to dry, throw on a very little flour and fry them brown in butter, then put to them some gravy, a little red wine, pepper, cloves and mace, and let them stew a little, then roll a little butter in flour and toss them up. Put under roast mutton or lamb or serve them up alone or with eggs poached or boiled hard.

From Sandbeck, 19th century

STEWED PEAS

Put a quart of peas into a pan with an ounce of butter and plenty of cold water. Rub the peas and butter together until well mixed then pour off the water, and put the peas in a stewpan with a lettuce shred fine, one onion & a little parsley, a dessertspoon of sugar & a little salt. Let the peas stew half an hour. When done take out the onion & parsley. Mix one ounce of flour and butter together on a plate. Put into the peas and toss the whole over the fire until well mixed.

CANAPES AU LAITUE

Boil 6 eggs hard. Take out the yolks and pass them through a hair seive with half their quantity of butter and very little chilli & tarragon vinegar, pepper, salt and a little mustard.

Beat all to a cream.

Cut some thin slices of bread and coat both sides with the mixture. Put 2 slices together and put a lettuce leaf on each – prepare them gently and put away in a cool place till wanted. Then cut them in small pieces like sandwiches. This quantity is sufficient for about 8 persons.

From Bold Hall, 18th century

TO PRESERVE GREEN WALLNUTS

Take wallnuts before the shell is hard. Gather them on a dry day, boil them in water till they have lost their bitterness then put them in cold water & peel off the skin. Put them in a pan with their weight in sugar & as much water as will wet it. Boil them over a gentle fire; let them cool & boil them again & so do till they are enough. Put them in pots when cold, paper & bladder them.

TO STEW PIPPINS

Take the finest yellowest golden pippins, pare them very smoth and leave the dew bit on. Take a silver marrow spoon, and scope them of the stalk from the core and kernels as clean as you can, and throw them into water as you do them, then set them on a cool fire and keep turning them till they are a little soft. Then make a pretty good syrup, and boil them while they are tender. Cut a little lemon peel and boil in it to colour the syrup and lay a saucer over them to keep them under the syrup. If you do them 2 or 3 days before you want to use them, they are better for lying in the syrup, but you must turn them in it every day. Then take a lemon, pare it and cut it with a pair of sissers as narrow as you can all the length and throw it in the syrup and when you serve them up throw the peel over them. If you think ye syrup too sweet squeeze in the juice of a lemon when you serve them to table.

TO PRESERVE PEACHES
OR APRICOTS IN BRANDY

Put your peaches in boiling water and just give them a scald but do not boil them. Take them out and wipe them dry and put them upon a seive, then put them into close jars and to seal peaches take a quarter of a pound of clarify'd sugar, pour it over your peaches just warm and then fill up either the jars or bottles which the peaches are in with brandy and stop them close.

THE BEST JELLY OF CURRANTS

Take 4 pounds of currants and 3 lb of ye finest loaf sugar. Wet your sugar and boil it to sugar again. Pick your currants of the stalkes and put them into the pan and let it stand till the sugar is wet, then set it over the fire till the sugar is melted. But do not let it boil. Put it thro a seive and let the clear jelly be put into glasses and the whole currants reserved in pots for tarts. They make better tarts than if the juice was all in them.

NB. but I am not in that opinion for unless you put some sugar to them they are very dry.

From Tring Park
in the Sandbeck Collection

POT POURI

1 Pound dried Rose Leaves	½ Pound dried Verbena Leaves
¾ Pound dried Lavender Flowers	½ oz. each of dried Thyme & Mint

These leaves should all be picked fresh and dried in the sun.

When quite dry they should be mixed with the following spices which must be pounded fine in a mortar.

½ oz. Cloves
½ oz. Nutmeg
½ oz. Mace
½ oz. Cinnamon
½ lb. Orris Root
1 oz. Rock Salt and a small quantity Musk Grain

Household duties

Until the Tudor aristocracy built their palaces there was not a great deal to clean in the country mansion. The housemaid has had her work cut out ever since. She is still, in her new guise of the daily cleaning woman, the last permanent indoors servant left in many a household.

Until the present century the manor houses made their own cleaning materials. Floors were washed with various substances from strong lye water to a scrub with sand or brick dust. Slate floors were polished to a raven's wing gloss with mutton fat. The yellow-painted floors of New England have their origin in the yellow stoning used to polish sandstone slab floors. Carpets were brightened with a vinegar rub and cleaned with damp tea-leaves, scattered over the pile and then swept up. Windows were washed with vinegar diluted in rainwater, and polished with a dab of paraffin on a soft cloth. By 1810 the housemaid had a supply of Goddards Silver Cleaner, and in 1876 a Bissell carpet sweeper, imported from America. The London engineer James Booth invented the vacuum cleaner in 1901. His machines were immediately patronized by royalty and Queen Alexandra had them installed at Buckingham Palace. The Hoover company of the United States set up shop in Britain in 1919.

Care of the laundry and linen closet has always been an important household duty. Soap remained a precious commodity and a favourite item for taxation until the early nineteenth century, when a cheap way of manufacturing soda was discovered and soap became widely available commercially. The aristocracy stopped using lye and did their washing in soap from about 1850. Although William Baillie built a somewhat cumbersome prototype washing machine and published its specifications in 1758, the machine, modified somewhat, was not produced and marketed for a hundred years. The large country households, with their quantities of linen and servants, were pioneer users. Some of the early machines were steam-powered, but electrical washing machines began to be installed in the 1920s when country houses received electricity supplies. Victorian laundry maids used flat irons (heavy metal instruments warmed on a stove) or box irons (hollowed to accommodate charcoal or hot metal), which remained in use until after World War II. Victorian irons were purpose-built, with different shapes for different jobs. For frills there were goffering irons – instruments much like curling-tongs which produced a fluted effect for edges and collars.

One of the most essential duties of the mistress of the household was the care of the health of her family, servants and dependants. The following group of recipes includes a number of traditional remedies and medicines.

From Bold Hall, 18th century

TO MAKE A SALINE DRAUGHT

Take 1½ oz of salt of wormwood, squease 2 lemons upon it, keep it stirring, add a pint and half of boiling water to it and a little brandy or cinimon water to warme it. This quantity makes 14 doses.

FOR THE AGUE

Best Peruve Bark in fine powder, half an ounce salt of tarter, 1 dram alum finely powdered, 1 seruple, 1 large nutmeg put into a pint of ale. To be divided into 6 doses.

A RECEIPT FOR A SORE THROAT
OR LUMP IN THE THROAT

To one noggin of the juice of pounded nettle root, well strain'd, add rose water and white wine vinegar, each one spoonful. Put them into a tin saucepan over a good fire for about a quarter of an hour. Then set it by to cool and when you mean to use it, make it pretty warm and soak a strip of flannel in it, then scrape a little nutmeg over the wet flannel and apply it on the outside of the part affected. This you are to repeat twice in 24 hours, when it will most certainly complete the cure. Roll a strip of dry flannel over the one appli'd to the part.

CHALK JULEP

Take 1 oz of chalk, 2 drams of gum arabic. 6 drams of fine sugar, 2 oz of nutmeg water.

FOR ONE WHO HAS DROPSICAL SYMPTOMS

Lay a quart of broom ashes upon a thin cloth over a large earthen pan. Pour upon it gently one gallon of the best mountain wine, warm and pass it a second time thro the ashes, then add half an ounce of nutmeg, two ounces of mustard seed, both brusd, and a large handfull of scrap'd horse radish. Let it all infuse 48 hours in a jug, close stopp'd. Stir it up every night that it may settle before you drink it in the morning. When it is half out pour the rest of the ingredients. Of this liquor drink a large coffee cupfull going to bed, another before you rise, as much at dinner and supper. If you find it too much in the morning, omit the morning draught and take more at your dinner, but you must not drink any other liquid whatsoever, nor eat any bread but dry toast. Doctr. Alcock says there should be added 2 ounces of brus'd juniper burrys, half an ounce of saffron, an ounce of fresh lemon peel and half an ounce of dry'd orange peel. He prefers a gallon of ale to mountain wine.

THE PURGE

To one quart of the best brandy put two ounces of jallup in powder, infuse it in a bottle shaking it well the day before you take it that it may have time to settle. Of this take as much as you find you can bear every other day till the destemper abaites, then once in 3 or 4 days. When the physick is taken the dish drink must be omitted, except a little at dinner & veal or mutton broth will be most proper.

FOR THE WORMES

Fenagrich, turmarick, aniseed & aloes of each 1d. to be pounded and put in treacle. A teaspoonfull for a child.

BROTH FOR SICK OR WEAK PEOPLE

Take 1 lb of lean beef or mutton or both together to all put 2 quarts of water, skim the meat, and take off all the fat, then cut it into little pieces and boil it till it comes to a quarter of a pint, season with a little common salt, skim off all the fat and give a spoonful of this broth at a time to very weak people, half a spoonful is enough to some, a teaspoonful, a teacupfull twice a day is the largest quantity ever taken.

THE FAMOUS AMERICAN RECEIPT FOR THE RHEUMATISM
WHITEHALL EVENING POST

Take of garlic two cloves, of gum armoniac one drachm, blend them by bruising them together; make them into three bolusses, with fair water & swallow them, one at night, and one in the morning drink while taking this receipt sassafras tea, made very strong, so as to have the teapot filled with chips. This is generally found to banish the rhumatism & even contractions of the joints in a few times taking. It is very famous in America and a hundred pounds have been given for the receipt.

FOR THE GRAVEL

Take the claws of bacon hogs and dry them in the sun upon pewter plates. Then fix them in a vice and rasp them with a file. Sift the powder through a muslin sieve and take as much as will lye upon a shilling in a little barley water or water when the fit is upon you, and if that don't do take another dose in half an hour and so on till the pain is remov'd.

TO CURE A CANCER

Rub the part affected with the juice of hemlock twice a day till a supparation takes place and whilst rubbing the opening, physic must be taken twice or three times a week. The patient is able to drink a quart at least of new milk wey every day & to live very obstemiously the whole time.

A RECEPE FOR DEAFNESS

Half an ounce of Hungary Water & the same of camphorated spirit of wine, with ten drops of the spirit of lavander. Rub this behind the ears & upon the temples every night and morning.

AN EFFECTUAL & IMMEDIATE CURE, EVEN IN THE MOST DESPERATE CASES, FOR CATTLE THAT HAVE OVERFED THEMSELVES IN WET CLOVER

Take an egg, empty the shell, fill it with tar. Throw it unbroken down the throat of the creature; 'tho ready to burst, within less than five minutes, the swelling will be abated and the danger entirely over.

DOCTOR ALCOCK'S PRESCRIPTION FOR A STRAIN

Take of camphire one drachm, dissolve it in an ounce of the Athereal Spirit of Turpentine, then add volatile liniment, Saponaceous Liniment, of each one ounce, these to be very well mixt into liniment.

THIEVES VINEGAR

Take rue, sage, mint, lavender & wormwood of each one handful. Chop it small, infuse it in a pint of wine vinegar, close stopped, near the fire (if it be in winter) two or three days, if in summer a week by the sun does better. Then strain it out and dissolve in it an ounce of camphire, broke in small pieces, which won't melt unless it is often shook. Rub your lips and nostrils with it. In towns and places full of infection it will be necessary to do more, to make your whole body and cloaths smell of it. A memorable story, when the Plague was last at Marseilles, gave credit to this recipe, but a more rational recommendation of it is that in air filled with the scent of such a mixture, the Animalculi, or infuting effluvia, that fly off with the air from diseased Pestilential Bodies, cannot live.

FOR LOW NERVOUS PEOPLE

DR FOTHERGILL

Spirit of lavender, tincture of castor, salvolatile in equal quantities. To take a teaspoonful at eleven o'clock in the morning and at six o'clock in the evening.

AN INFALLIBLE CURE FOR
ALL SCROPHULOUS DISORDERS

From the St James's Chronicle

Common aqua vitae, or brandy 20 ounces, of fixed volatile Alkali Concrete and gentian root, otherwise called Felnort or Balmody, of each one drachm and a half. Let these infuse in the liquor for the space of 24 hours before you use it, and let it remain on the Root, as it will get strength the more it is in that situation, the dose is fasting before dinner and supper, at each time a tablespoonfull.

RECEIPT FOR THE ITCH WITHOUT MEDECINE

LADY JANE STANLEY

Pomatum half an ounce, milk of brimstone three drachms, balsam of sulphur made with oil of turpentine thirty drops, oil of Rhodium nine drops, oil of sweet almonds a sufficient quantity to make it up into an ointment.

Take the size of a nut of this ointment, lay it on the palm of the hand, rub the hands together & frequently smell to it, when that quantity is rubb'd dry add a little more.

Let this be done every night till the whole is used. Half the above quantity of ingredients is enough to cure one who has not a very inveterate confirmed itch. Be sure you have the true oil of Rhodium, much depends on it.

LORD CHESTERFIELD'S RECEIPT FOR SCURVY IN THE FACE

who never knew it fail, if persisted in

Take 5 ounces of raisins of the sun, chop them very fine, put them into a pint of skim milk. Let it simmer over the fire till it is reduced to half the quantity. Break it into whey with the juice of a Seville orange or lemon if no orange can be had. Drink it next morning fasting.

SOAP PILLS FOR BILE

DR BARRY

Nine drams of Castile soap and three of rhubarb mix'd up with syrup of saffron and made into 40 pills.

FOR WORMS

MY SISTER HESKETH

An handful of tansey, do. of wormwood, an ounce of bark, a quart of boiling water pour'd upon it and strain it off the next day, and a pint of water may be pour'd upon the ingredients. The dose: a small wine glass.

A DAILY WASH FOR YE TEETH

A quart of port wine, put to it an ounce of Bol Armoniac, half an oz Myrrh, one drachm of Allum, an ounce of Hungary water, 10 grains of salt of vitriol & two ounces of honey of roses. Let these stand in a warm oven or near a fire for three days. Set them by to settle and pour a tablespoonful of it into a teacup of water with which wash the mouth well. It preserves ye teeth sound, and the gums free from scurvy.

4

Special Occasions

These are among the particular pleasures of country house life: the shooting lunches, nursery teas, hunting breakfasts and theatre suppers have been, and still are, enjoyed by generations of country households.

The menus in the following section have all been contributed by the various houses to which the recipes are credited. All of them are in current use in the owners' own kitchens.

Dining in Scotland

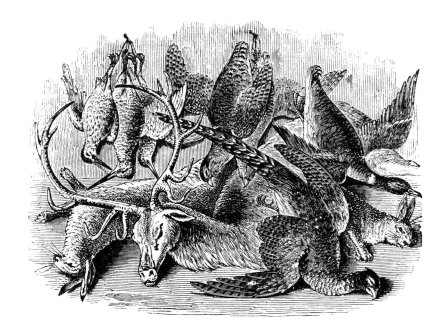

From William Dunbar's *Dirige to the King at Stirling*, *circa* 1500, on the
pleasures of an invitation to dine at the palace of Holyrood:

> To eit swan, cran, pertik and plever,
> And every fische that swymis in rever;
> To drynke with ws the new fresche wyne,
> That grew upon the rever of Ryne,
> ffresche, fragrant clairettis out of France,
> Of Angerss and of Orliance,
> With mony and courss of grit dyntie;
> Say yc amen, for cheritie.

From General Sir Ian Hamilton's autobiography, *When I was a Boy*, 1939:

In the kitchen, a huge sirloin of beef or, at the least, a gigot from a four-year-old black-faced sheep, late of the far-famed Hafton [his home in Argyllshire] flock, would be revolving slowly on the main spit before the fire . . .

A few years ago my brother Vereker, wishing to refresh his memory, asked my Aunt Camilla (who at the time happened to have another very old lady staying with her) – 'Wasn't it the case that at dinner there were always four covered dishes laid, one at each corner of the table, as well as those at the top and bottom?' Both the old ladies held up their hands and exclaimed with one voice – '*And* the side dishes!' Yes, there were the side dishes. That made eight dishes in all. Today it will seem to be too strange to be true, but it is true, though some of them may have held only vegetables. Always there was either haggis or sheep's head at the foot of the table; that was *de rigueur*; and always one of the corner dishes was curry and rice. A turkey, a goose, or a haunch of roe-deer venison, or some such flea-bite was somewhere for sure. There were no such things as hors-d'oeuvre, but before the heavy stuff there had been of course soup and fish – real fish – none of your flabby stuff from off the ice at the fishmonger's, but freshly caught in sea or river by the estate fishermen, great heroes and friends to us children. After this came eight sweets. Cream was handed round with all the sweets which had to be eaten with a spoon and not with a fork as in England.

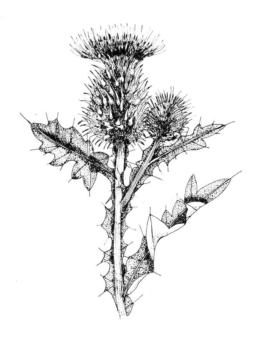

Lady Lovat's recipes
from Balblair House, Invernesshire

Crème Lorraine
Woodcock Pudding for winter
Carrots with parsley
Creamed potatoes
Tulipes

CRÈME LORRAINE

Serves 6

¼ lb (1 cup) grated cheese
(gruyère and parmesan in equal quantities)
½ pt (1¼ cups) cream
1 egg
salt and cayenne pepper

Mix the cheese and cream together, add the egg, well-beaten, a pinch of salt and cayenne pepper. Stir well and pour the mixture into little soufflé dishes (one for each person). Cook carefully in a *bain marie* in a fairly hot oven. Serve with hot toast.

This is rather a rich first course and we usually follow with a plain roast meat or a roast grouse.

WOODCOCK PUDDING FOR WINTER

Serves 4

4 woodcock de-boned, kidneys and liver
1 can Baxter's Royal Game Soup or stock
1 medium onion, sliced
glass red wine
seasoning

Dip the de-boned breast, legs, kidney and liver of the woodcock in seasoned flour. Fry for a few minutes in hot fat to seal the pieces. Place in a pudding basin. Cook the onions to brown. Place with the woodcock. Cover the meat and onions with the red wine and soup or stock. Season well. Cover the top of the basin with a suet paste. Tie up with a cloth. Steam for 1½ to 2 hours. Decorate with a woodcock beak before serving.

We would start dinner with a sliver or two of smoked salmon, and after the woodcock pudding, we would serve Athol brose (a mixture of whisky, oatmeal and honey).

TULIPES

Serves 4

3½ oz (½ cup) double cream
3½ oz (¾ cup) icing sugar
3½ oz (¾ cup) plain flour

Mix together all the ingredients in a bowl, then spread very thin on greased baking sheets, having cut into circles (about 4 inches across). Smooth flat with the back of a spoon. Bake in the oven at 350°F, 180°C, Reg. 4 for 10–12 minutes. As soon as the tulipes leave the oven, they must be quickly shaped in small moulds and allowed to cool. They must either be kept very dry or done at the last minute as they otherwise lose their crispness. They can be filled with fruit ice cream or whipped cream, but as an alternative, condensed milk makes a more original filling. To prepare it, take 1 tin of Nestlés condensed milk and boil it unopened in hot water for 1 hour. Then open the tin and spoon the contents into the tulipes.

Shooting lunches

LAMBTON PARK

VARIOUS

From *Kitchen Essays* (1922) by Lady Jekyll, food correspondent of *The Times*:

Some suggestions, neither novel nor elaborate, since the occasion hardly calls for such, but possibly of use to hostess or cook beset by many conflicting claims, are offered. For the main dish a big brown marmite, piping hot from a hay-box, or warmed up on the cottage fire, the contents fresh neck of mutton or lamb, with potatoes and small pickling onions; or, alternatively, a hotpot of game or poultry with celery, peeled chestnuts, and a milky gravy, flavoured with Worcester sauce or mushrooms, together with a bowl of jacketed potatoes and a casserole of baked Boston beans . . . Jam or spiced apple puffs, covered-in cheesecakes or mince-pies, are an easy second course to serve and consume; while a little truckle cheese or wedge of Gruyère, with butter and lettuces or celery, and a tin of mixed plain biscuits hotted up and crisp in their tin home, and a sportsman cake should be included.

Mr Henry Keswick's recipes from Hunthill, Angus

Mrs Gibbs' butterfly venison
Red cabbage
Mrs Gibbs' clootie dumpling

MRS GIBBS' BUTTERFLY VENISON

Serves 8–10

1 haunch of venison carefully boned out, leaving long and short sides
9 tablespoons olive oil
3 tablespoons wine vinegar
1 teaspoon dry mustard
1 teaspoon sugar
salt and pepper

Cut right through the short side of the haunch and you will now have a flat piece of meat resembling the shape of a butterfly. Trim if necessary.

Into a jar with a lid put the olive oil, wine vinegar, mustard and sugar, and season with salt and black pepper to taste. Shake well and pour over venison. Marinate for at least 24 hours, turning the venison from time to time. If your haunch is fairly big, you may need a little more marinade.

Heat a grill till very hot (or very hot oven). Put the meat cut side up under the grill and cook till brown and crisp; turn and grill the other side till brown and crisp. Reduce the heat to half, and cook for a further 20–30 minutes each side. Remove the meat on to a hot platter and make a gravy with the juices from the meat, adding a little port if wished. Serve with roast or baked potatoes and red cabbage.

RED CABBAGE

Take 1 red cabbage, finely sliced into thin strips, 1 lb onions, sliced, 1 lb cooking apples, sliced, 1 teaspoon salt, 10 turns of black pepper, 4 tablespoons brown sugar, 1 teaspoon marjoram, ½ teaspoon ground mace, ¼ teaspoon ground cloves, 1 clove garlic, crushed (optional), 2 red pimentos, thinly sliced, piece of orange peel, ½ pt (1¼ cups) red wine and wine vinegar

Into a deep casserole, layer the cabbage, onion and apple, seasoning with the spices and other ingredients (except the wine and vinegar) as you go along. Moisten with the wine and vinegar, cover and cook in a slow oven (300°F, 150°C, Reg. 2) for about 3 hours.

MRS GIBBS' CLOOTIE DUMPLING

This recipe won the East of Scotland Championship

8 oz (2 cups) plain flour
pinch of salt
2 oz (4 tbsp) suet
2 oz (¼ cup) castor sugar
(plus enough to sprinkle over the dumpling after it is cooked)
½ teaspoon each of ground ginger, mixed spice and bicarbonate of soda
1 egg
1 rounded tablespoon treacle
milk to mix
12 oz/1 lb (3 cups) raisins
(or a mixture of dried fruits, but I only use raisins)

Put a large pan of water on to boil with a heatproof plate in the bottom. Sift the flour with a pinch of salt and rub in the suet lightly. Add the sugar, spices and soda. Beat the egg and add to the dry ingredients with the treacle. Mix, adding enough milk to make a fairly stiff consistency. Add the raisins and mix all well together. Scald a linen cloth, flour well and spoon the mixture into the centre. Gather up the folds of cloth and tie with string. Put into a pan of boiling water and boil steadily for 3 hours. Take out and put into a colander. Carefully untie the string and pull back the cloth as much as you can. Put a serving plate on top of the dumpling and turn everything over, colander and all. First take off the colander, then, carefully, the cloth, taking care not to break the skin of the dumpling. Serve hot with castor sugar and pouring cream.

NB. The mixture is more easily spooned into the cloth if the cloth is first put into a bowl. In Scotland, the dumpling is often served cold and cut into slices as a cake, or cut into fairly thin slices and fried lightly in butter and again served with sugar and cream.

Irish dinners

From *The Tour of a German Prince*, London, 1832:

Our hunt did not end till the approach of twilight. It had become excessively cold, and the flickering fire, with the table spread before it, shone most agreeably upon us at our arrival at Captain S's house. A genuine sportsman's and batchelor's feast followed. There was no attempt at show or elegance. Glasses, dishes, and all the furniture of the table, were of every variety of form and date: one man drank his wine out of a liqueur glass: another out of a champagne glass, the more thirsty out of tumblers. One ate with his great-grandfather's knife and fork, his neighbour with a new green-handled one which the servant had just bought at Cashel fair. There were as many dogs as guests in the room: every man waited on himself; and the meats and potables were pushed on the table in abundance by an old woman and a heavy-fisted groom.

The fare was by no means to be despised, nor the wine either, nor the poteen

---

clandestinely distilled in the mountains which I have tasted for the first time genuine and unadulterated. For sweetening a pudding, two large lumps of sugar were handed about, and we rubbed them together as the savages do sticks for kindling fire. That the drinking was on a vast an unlimited scale you may safely presume; but though many at last could not speak very articulately, yet no one attempted anything indecorous or ill-bred . . . We rose from table very late.

Suggestions for an Irish dinner

from the Knight of Glin and Madam Fitzgerald

Glin fish pie
Guinness stew
Nancy Ellis's Irish stew
Mai Liston's summer pudding

GLIN FISH PIE

Serves 6–8

3 lb thick fresh cod or haddock
1 lb prawns, cooked and peeled
1 lb scallops, cooked
6 hard-boiled eggs
6 mushrooms, chopped
1 onion, grated
salt and pepper
a little grated cheese
1 cup breadcrumbs, browned

Cook the fish in milk. Reserving the milk for the sauce, flake the fish into the bottom of a casserole, then add a layer of prawns, next a layer of chopped mushrooms, next a layer of scallops, and then a layer of halved hard-boiled eggs. Make a white sauce with the milk. Add the onion, pepper and salt and a little grated cheese to this. Pour the sauce over the pie and top with the breadcrumbs. Bake for ¾ hour in an oven at 350°F, 180°C, Reg. 4.

GUINNESS STEW

Serves 8–10

4 lb good-quality stewing beef (cubed)
4 onions, chopped
1 lb streaky bacon, chopped
2 tablespoons brown sugar
2 tablespoons mustard
1 *bouquet garni*
1½ pt (3¾ cups) Guinness
cooking oil

Brown the meat in the pan and then add the onions and the streaky bacon. Cook together until the onion is golden, then add the brown sugar and mustard and the *bouquet garni*. Stir in all together, add the Guinness and bring to the boil. When boiling, pour into a casserole and cover securely. Cook in a medium oven for 2 hours. Take out and let cool overnight. Cook in a medium oven on the second day for another 2 hours.

Serve with small pieces of fried bread spread with mustard placed on the top of the stew, and sprinkle with fresh parsley.

NANCY ELLIS'S IRISH STEW

Serves 8–10

1 parsnip
8 small onions
6 medium-sized carrots
8 potatoes, peeled
4 lb rack of mutton chops
½ cup pearl barley (optional)
salt and pepper

It is essential that this dish is pre-cooked. Peel and cut up the parsnip, onions and carrots. Leave the chops whole. Put the onions, parsnip, carrots and chops into a large saucepan; cover with cold water. Add the pearl barley (if desired) and plenty of pepper and salt. On the first day, simmer for 1½ hours. Take off the heat and leave to cool overnight. The next morning, remove all the fat that will have congealed on the top. Bring to the boil and simmer for half an hour, adding the peeled potatoes. Sprinkle with chopped parsley before serving.

MAI LISTON'S SUMMER PUDDING

Serves 6

2 lb loganberries and/or raspberries
6 slices crustless white bread
½ lb (1 cup) sugar

For sauce:
1 lb blackcurrants
½ lb (1 cup) sugar

Wash the berries thoroughly and put them in a saucepan, with the sugar but no water. Simmer for 15 minutes. Line a soufflé dish with the bread cut into fingers. When the berries are cold, force them through a sieve and pour the resulting purée over the fingers of bread. Put any remaining bread fingers over the top and press a weighted saucer or plate on the top as a lid. Leave in refrigerator overnight.

For the sauce, put the blackcurrants, sugar and 2 cups of water into a saucepan and simmer for 10 minutes. Allow to cool, and pour over the summer pudding when serving. This is delicious with whipped cream.

Grouse moor picnics

The Revd Sydney Smith, the celebrated wit and founder, in 1802, of the *Edinburgh Review*:

No nation has so large a stock of benevolence of heart as the Scotch. Their temper stands anything but an attack on their climate. They would have you even believe they can ripen fruit; and, to be candid, I must own in remarkably warm summers I have tasted peaches that made excellent pickles.

The Duchess of Roxburghe's grouse moor picnic

Floors Castle, Roxburghshire

Grouse pâté (recipe follows)
Glazed lamb cutlets
Cold veal in breadcrumbs
Mixed salad
Jam puffs
Fruit cake
Stilton
Floury baps
Apple and chocolate
bar for the pocket

Further suggestions

EUSTON HALL

The Duchess of Grafton
Cauliflower soup

BALBLAIR

The Lady Lovat
Hare pâté
Cold game pie

BLAGDON

The Viscountess Ridley
Sloe gin

GROUSE PATE

Serves 8–10

2 young grouse
5 old grouse
6 oz (1½ cups) bacon pieces
1 small onion
4 oz (½ cup) butter
¼ pt (⅔ cup) double cream
2 tablespoons dry sherry
4 rashers steaky bacon

Pluck and prepare the grouse ready to roast. Roughly chop the bacon pieces and the onion. Sauté the bacon and onion in a roasting pan with half the butter. Put in the old grouse and baste; roast for 35 minutes at 375°F, 190°C, Reg. 5. Roast young grouse for 25 minutes at the same temperature. Leave to cool.

Remove all the meat from the old birds and mince finely with the bacon and onions from the roasting tin. Remove the meat from the young grouse in neat thin slices. Mix the cream and sherry into the minced grouse; season to taste. Butter the sides and base of a deep 1½ × 12 inch oval ovenproof dish. Divide the pâté mixture into thirds. Spread one-third over the bottom of the dish and lay on half of the slices of the young grouse; repeat, finishing with pâté on top. Lay the slices of streaky bacon on top of this, along with some freshly ground black pepper and small knobs of the remaining butter. Bake for 20 minutes in a fairly hot oven. Serve chilled.

CAULIFLOWER SOUP

THE DUCHESS OF GRAFTON'S RECIPE

Serves 6

1 oz (2 tbsp) butter
1 oz (¼ cup) flour
2 pt (5 cups) chicken stock
1 cauliflower
nutmeg
4 oz (½ cup) cream

Melt the butter, add the flour and enough stock to make a sauce. Add the rest of stock and cauliflower broken into florets. Bring to the boil and simmer for 20 minutes. Liquidize. Add the nutmeg to taste, and the cream just before serving.

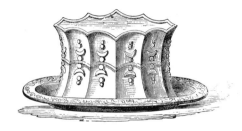

HARE PATE

6 oz (¾ cup) fat pork	salt and pepper
1 hare	1 lemon
1 egg	1 bay leaf
1 onion, chopped	butter

Mince the fat pork. Mince all the bits of hare from the rib bones, as well as the liver and the heart. Mix into this the egg and the onion, and pepper and salt to taste. Mix well together with your hands, adding the egg at the last.

Rub an ovenproof dish with lemon and pack the meat into the dish, but not too full because you must leave room for liquid. Cover with a layer of fat and a bay leaf. Cook in a slow oven for 2 hours.

Boil up the bones of the hare to make a good setting jelly, ready when the pâté is cooked. Pour into the dish. Allow the meat to cool for 24 hours without disturbing it. Seal with melted butter.

This pâté is also very good made with ham instead of hare.

COLD GAME PIE

2 lb venison, freed from all skin and sinew
1 lb deer's liver
salt and pepper
1 teaspoon finely chopped onion
bacon fat
1 deer's tongue
4 rashers of bacon
chopped parsley
½ pt (1¼ cups) venison stock

Mix together the venison, deer's liver, salt and pepper and onion and then pass through a mincing machine. Fry this in hot bacon fat and allow to cool. Simmer the deer's tongue in a saucepan with a few vegetables for about 1½ hours. Skin the tongue and cut into thin slices.

Place the rashers of bacon in the bottom of an ovenproof dish. Then add a layer of meat and liver. Sprinkle with a little chopped parsley and seasoning, then a layer of tongue, a layer of bacon and liver and so on until the dish is full. Add a breakfast cup of stock.

Cover the dish with a close fitting lid, stand it in a roasting tin containing an inch or two of water and cook in a moderate oven (350°F, 180°C, Reg. 4) for 2½ hours. While it is cooking, add more venison stock to keep it moist.

This dish can be improved by adding a glass of port wine to the stock, and you can also use other game as well as the venison.

We would use the cold game pie for a shooting lunch with hot baked potatoes, starting the luncheon with a good hot Scotch broth. We would also have a Stilton cheese and a sticky ginger cake to follow.

SLOE GIN

3½ lb sloes (picked *after* mid-October)   6 oz (1½ cups) sugar (or more to taste)
4 bottles of gin   almond essence

Mix the sloes, gin and sugar together into a large jar, shaking it frequently to ensure that all the sugar is dissolved. Leave for at least three months. Decant into bottles. Add 3 drops of almond essence to each bottle and mix.

Hunting breakfasts

From *The Tour of a German Prince*, London 1832:

A detailed description of this morning's breakfast will give you the best idea of the wants and the comfortable living of English travellers. NB. I had ordered nothing but tea. The following is what I found set out when I quitted my bedroom – in a little town scarcely so extensive as one of our villages.

In the middle of the table smoked a large tea-urn, prettily surrounded by silver tea-cannisters, a slop-basin, and a milk jug. There were three small Wedgwood plates, with as many knives and forks, and two large cups of beautiful porcelain: by them stood an inviting plate of boiled eggs, another 'ditto' of broiled *oreilles de cochon à la Sainte Menehould*, a plate of muffins, kept warm on a hot

---

water-plate; another with cold ham; flaky white bread, dry and buttered toast; the best fresh butter in an elegant glass vessel; convenient recepticles for salt and pepper, English mustard and *moutarde de maille*, lastly, a silver tea-caddy, with very good green and black tea.

Menu for a hunting breakfast

TICHBORNE PARK

Lady Jekyll's 1920 recipe for 'Chasse'
Salmon Kedgeree

ASKE, YORKSHIRE

The Marchioness of Zetland
Penelope's brown scones

SANDBECK PARK

Mrs Dowse's orange marmalade
(a 19th century recipe)

LADY JEKYLL'S 1920 RECIPE FOR 'CHASSE'

Serves 3–4

1 onion, chopped
6 tomatoes
1 slice of ham
3 potatoes
2 oz (½ cup) grated cheese
pinch of paprika
pinch of allspice
3–8 eggs

Fry the onion lightly in a buttered sauté pan. Add the skinned tomatoes and ham, both cut up small. When these are well browned, add a little water and the diced potatoes, and cook slowly till these are done. Before serving, mix in the grated cheese, slightly flavoured with paprika and allspice, till the mixture is ropy. Pour on to a hot dish, and serve with a nicely poached egg on the top, one or two for each person. If preferred, omit the cheese.

SALMON KEDGEREE

Serves 4

1 lb salmon
1 pt (2½ cups) milk
8 oz (1 cup) long-grain rice

½ lb (1 cup) butter
4 chopped hard-boiled eggs
½ pt (1¼ cups) cream

Poach the salmon in the milk and an equal amount of water. When it is done, flake the fish, carefully removing the bones. Cook the rice in the liquid in which you have poached the fish. When it is done, rinse it under warm water. Melt the butter in a large saucepan. Add the rinsed rice and mix in the flaked salmon, chopped eggs, cream and a generous screw of black pepper. Warm up slowly and serve.

PENELOPE'S BROWN SCONES

THE MARCHIONESS OF ZETLAND'S RECIPE

Makes about 12

1 oz (2 tbsp) soft brown sugar
¼ pt (⅔ cup) milk
8 oz (2 cups) self-raising wholewheat flour
1½ oz (3 tbsp) margarine or butter
a little extra milk for the glaze

Dissolve the sugar in the milk. Put the flour in a basin and rub in the butter. Add the sugar and milk and knead into a dough. Roll a thickness of ½ inch, cut with a 2½ in cutter and put into an oven preheated to 450°F, 230°C, Reg. 8, for 20 minutes.

MRS DOWSE'S ORANGE MARMALADE

It is better to weigh the oranges whole. Put 1 lb sugar to 1 lb oranges.

First take off the peel of the oranges, put it into cold water and boil it until quite tender. Take it up on to a seive to drain all night. Scrape out all the pulp of the oranges and take away all seeds and strings. Then cut the peel very thin. Put the sugar into a preserving pan, and just damp it with cold water. When the sugar has boiled quite clear, put in the pulp and boil a quarter of an hour, then add the peel and boil altogether 20 minutes, not fast, only simmer or it is apt to candy.

Nursery teas

From Charlotte Brontë, *Jane Eyre* (1847):

'Mr Rochester would be glad if you and your pupil would take tea with him in the drawing-room this evening,' said she [Mrs Fairfax] . . . 'He has been so much engaged all day that he could not ask to see you before.'

'When is his tea-time?' I inquired.

'Oh, at six o'clock: he keeps early hours in the country. You had better change your frock now, I will go with you and fasten it. Here is a candle.'

'Is it really necessary to change my frock?'

'Yes, you had better: I always dress for the evening when Mr Rochester is here.'

From Mrs Adrian Secker of Bridgefoot, Iver, Bucks., a contemporary account of a nursery tea:

In my nursery there was a coal fire with a high guard. Nanny had the kettle on the hob, and made toast for us. We had toast and dripping and Guard's cake (I once ate seven slices of this and was sick).

When I was four, Nanny left; my brother went to prep school and I was entrusted to a governess. My mother came to tea in the nursery if she had nothing better to do. I remember her horror when she saw Mam'zelle lick her fingers and pick up the crumbs off her plate with her wet finger.

My own children have always had tea in the kitchen. The best tip I got was from Cliveden, where we had 'French toast'.

Nursery tea recipes

BRIDGEFOOT

French toast
Queen cakes
Guard's cake
Mrs Fox's gingerbread
Dough cake

SANDBECK

Brethy sandwiches
(a 19th century recipe)

FRENCH TOAST

Butter some bread, and place on a frying pan *butter side* down; the heat of the flame pulls the butter up through the bread. Delicious, and surprisingly little mess. Cinnamon, meat or yeast extracts or patum peperium (Gentleman's Relish) may be added.

QUEEN CAKES

Small round sponge cakes, known as queen cakes if they have sultanas in, and butterfly cakes if they have the tops cut off, bisected, and popped back at an angle with a little jam or cream, to form 'wings'.

4 oz (½ cup) butter or margarine
4 oz (½ cup) castor sugar
2 eggs
4 oz (1 scant cup) self-raising flour
a little milk
2 oz (4 tbsp) sultanas

Brush tartlet tins with melted lard. Cream the butter and sugar. Add the eggs with a spoonful of flour. Fold in the rest of the flour, and add enough milk to soften. Mix in the sultanas. Half-fill the tins. Bake at 400°F, 205°C, Reg. 8 for 15–20 minutes.

GUARD'S CAKE

12 oz (3 cups) flour
6 oz (¾ cup) margarine
4 oz (½ cup) currants
2 oz (4 tbsp) peel (optional)
4 oz (½ cup) sultanas
4 oz (1 scant cup) brown sugar
1 teaspoon ground ginger
1 teaspoon mixed spice
1 teaspoon cream of tartar
1 teaspoon bicarbonate of soda
pinch of salt

Rub the flour and margarine together. Add the other ingredients and mix well with milk (rather slack). Bake in a moderate to slow oven for 2 hours.

MRS FOX'S GINGERBREAD

4 oz (½ cup) butter
9 oz (1 cup) treacle
4 oz (½ cup) sugar
10 oz (2¾ cups) self-raising flour
½ teaspoon salt
1 teaspoon ground ginger
1 teaspoon cinnamon
1 beaten egg
8 fl. oz (1 cup) yoghurt

Use 7-inch-square paper-lined tin.

Melt the butter, treacle and sugar in a saucepan and allow to cool. Sift together the flour, salt, and spices. Make a well in the centre and add the treacle mixture, the egg and the yoghurt. Beat well, pour into the prepared cake tin and bake for 1 hour, 20 minutes at 325°F, 170°C, Reg. 3.

DOUGH CAKE

1½ lb (4½ cups) mixed fruit
½ lb (1 cup) demerara sugar
¾ pt (2 cups) cold Indian tea, strained
1 egg
1 lb (4 cups) self-raising flour

Soak the fruit and sugar in the tea overnight. The next day, stir in the egg and the flour. Divide the mixture into 2 greased loaf tins. Bake at 350°F, 180°C, Reg. 4 for 1½ hours.

BRETHY SANDWICHES

Cut up into dice some chicken, ham or tongue, truffles, a few capers or gherkins and a hard-boiled egg and some mustard and cress. Mix with a little tartare sauce. Put between rounds of bread and butter and serve on cress.

The Coming of Age
of Viscount Lumley, 1878

The coming of age of the eldest son is still a big event for the British landed aristocracy – involving tents, tenants, toasts, relations, lunches, dinners, speeches, drink – for he will be the next in charge. Today though, the celebrations are perhaps not quite as elaborate or long-drawn-out as in the nineteenth century. The coming of age of Viscount Lumley in 1878 lasted from Saturday 16th November till Wednesday 27th November. And the festivities at Sandbeck and Lumley are minutely recorded in a 25-page red leather book.

Some of the exhaustive lists of those present, the expenses, entertainments and comestibles, are reproduced in the following pages. The rest is a verbose but marvellous description of each day's happenings. Lord Lumley entertained tenants from four estates: Sandbeck in Yorkshire, Glentworth, Lumley and Stainton. The phenomenal amount of organisation is self-evident and the cost appreciable if the grand total of £4000 is multiplied by 30 to reach a rough modern equivalent.

Tuesday 19th November was the high point. The tenants, represented by a Mr Crawford, presented Viscount Lumley with a splendid sword and the former read an adulatory address. This was followed by an equally flowery address on behalf of the tradesmen and others on the estate, read by Mr John Clark, the ex-mayor of Doncaster.

> [Their present was] 'a magnificent canteen service, supplied by Messrs. Mappin and Webb, of Sheffield and London. It consisted of a handsome bound oak case, on which a shield engraved with his lordship's crest. Inside, the chest was fitted with trays containing 2 dozen ivory table knives, 1½ dozen ivory dessert knives, 1 pair ivory 8-inch carvers, 1 pair ivory 9-inch carvers, 1 pair ivory game

carvers, 1 ivory steel, 2 dozen table forks, 1½ dozen dessert forks, 1 dozen table spoons, 1½ dozen dessert spoons, 1 dozen tea spoons, ½ dozen egg spoons, ⅓ dozen salt spoons, mustard spoon, 1 soup ladle, 4 sauce ladles, 2 gravy spoons, 1 pair sugar tongs, 1 butter knife, 1 case fish carvers, 2 breakfast cruets, 2 pair nutcracks, 1 marrow spoon, 1 butter dish, 1 toast rack, 1 salver 8-inch, 1 salver 12-inch, 1 cheese scoop, 1 dozen fruit desserts, 6 napkin rings, 1 pair grape scissors, and 4 salt cellars, all bearing his Lordship's crest.

After receiving the address, Viscount Lumley advanced to the table on which the canteen was displayed, and, after the cheering had subsided, said:

'Gentlemen, I thank you very sincerely for this your very beautiful present. I assure you I appreciate most highly the very great honour you have done me to-day, and am deeply grateful for the congratulations which have just been addressed to me, not excepting the very valuable gift, this handsome service, which will be most useful to me at home, and possibly abroad, if the need should arise. (Hear, hear, and cheers.) I thank you, gentlemen, from the bottom of my heart.' (Loud cheers.)

Then the 400 guests sat down to dinner (sic) at 2.30 pm. The tent was adorned with flags, flowers, magnificent plate, and they ate:

Queue de Boeuf. Tortue fausse clair.
Côtelettes de mouton aux pois. Venaison rotie. Faisans. Perdrix.
Baron of beef.
Pâté de gibier. Jambon au vin de Champagne. Langue de boeuf a l'écarlate.
Poulets. Dindon farcie aux truffes. Salades de homard à la russe. Gelées.
Pâtisserie. Gâteaux. Meringue.
Plum puddings.

THE
COMING OF AGE
OF
VISCOUNT LUMLEY.

Details of the Festivities which took place at Sandbeck, Lumley, Glentworth, and Stainton.

DATES. 1878. November and December.	Family.	Gentry from Yorkshire, Nottinghamshire, &c.	Tenant Farmers and Tradespeople and their Families on Sandbeck, Lumley and Lincolnshire Estates.	Workpeople and Small Tenants and their Families on Sandbeck, Lumley and Lincolnshire Estates.	Children on the Sandbeck and Lumley Estates.	Waiters, Attendants, and Household.	Musicians.	Policemen.	Coachmen and Grooms.	Daily Total.
Monday, 18th November ...	28	250	—	—	—	130	12	10	144	574
Tuesday, 19th ,, ...	28	40	600	—	—	130	42	10	100	950
Wednesday, 20th ,, ...	28	20	—	600	—	130	42	10	35	865
Thursday, 21st ,, ...	20	30	—	—	700	100	30	10	18	908
Tuesday, 26th ,, (Lumley)	3	1	250	—	—	25	23	4	10	316
Wednesday, 27th ,, ,,	3	1	—	—	1,200	20	16	4	4	1,248
Wednesday, 4th December (Stainton and Glentworth)	—	—	—	210	—	12	4	—	—	226
TOTALS	110	342	850	810	1,900	547	169	48	311	5,087

NUMBER OF PERSONS PRESENT.

PROVISIONS, FRUIT, WINES, BEER, &c.,

Used during the Festivities.

		£	s.	d.
3	Oxen			
25	Sheep			
	Suet, Veal, Lard, Ham, Bacon			
16	Haunches Venison . .			
16	Necks do. . .			
90	Pheasants . .			
165	Partridges and Grouse ,			
300	Fowls			
	Pigeons, Ducks, Geese, &c.			
114	Rabbits			
	Tongues (Ox and Reindeer), Cheese, Butter, Eggs . . .			
80	Pints Cream . . .			
336	Quarts Milk . . .			
	Salmon, Lobsters, &c. .			
	Flour, Bread, Buns, and Cakes			
	Tea, Sugar, and Sundry Groceries . . .			
12	Bushel Potatoes . .			
1	Do. Onions . .			
4	Do. Apples and Pears			

Carried forward £

		£	s.	d.
	Brought forward			
100	lb. Grapes . . .			
92	Beets			
98	Cucumbers . . .			
350	Lettuce . . , .			
560	Cauliflowers . . .			
	Pine Apples, Melons, Figs, Raisins, &c. .			
	Champagne . . .			
	Port, Sherry, Claret, Brandy, Whisky, Gin, Beer			
	Seltzer Water, Soda Water, and Lemonade . .			
	Cigars and Tobacco .			
	Provisions for Banquet and other Entertainments at Lumley . .			
	Dinner and Tea for Workmen and small Tenants at Glentworth and Stainton . . .			
	Amounting in all to the sum of . . £1,311	12	7

AMUSEMENTS, FIREWORKS, &c.

Provided for the Festivities.

Description.	£	s.	d.
Punch and Judy	8	10	0
Band of 1st West York Yeomanry Cavalry	76	9	0
Lumley Brass Band	12	0	0
THOS. THRUSH's String Band	44	10	0
T. A. HUNTER's do.	4	15	0
Bell Ringers	3	10	0
Prizes at Athletic Sports, &c.	11	10	6
	£161	4	6

Messrs. BROCK and Co., Display of Fireworks, Illuminations, Salute of Guns, &c. £205 5 0

ACCOMMODATION, &c.

	£	s.	d.
Mr. BENJAMIN EDGINGTON, 2, Duke Street, London Bridge—For Tents, Decorations, Lighting, &c.	690	2	8
Carriage of Tents, Chairs, Fireworks, Plate, Cutlery, and all Stores .	400	11	6
Messrs. GUNTER & CO., London—Hire of Plate, &c. . . .	300	0	0
Messrs. MAWE & SON—Hire of Beds, &c. . . .	159	7	8
Lodgings for Tenants from Lincolnshire and Durham Estates—			
Mr. J. T. DOOLEY	26	17	9
Mrs. SPITTLEHOUSE	1	1	0
Mr. PARKIN	1	1	0
Mr. MURRAY	5	9	0
Mr. WHINFREY	1	4	0
Mr. WHITE	6	12	6
Mr. TURNELL	1	4	0
Mr. COLLIER	5	15	0
Carried forward	£1,599	6	1

ACCOMMODATION, &c.—*continued.*

	£	s.	d.
Brought forward	1,599	6	1
Carriage Hire, &c.—			
Messrs. SMITH & SON, Doncaster	82	1	0
Mr. W. H. Pye, do.	2	7	6
Mr. WHITE, Bawtry	13	3	c
Mr. TAYLOR, Retford	3	10	0
Mr. COLLIER, Tickhill	9	10	0
Mr. NEALE, Worksop	0	18	0
Mr. BURN, Chester-le-Street	4	2	0
Messrs. FISHER, HOLMES & CO., Plants	37	5	9
Invitation Cards, Printing, &c.	25	10	8
Mr. J. SLACK, Straw	7	10	0
Mr. E. WILMSHURST, Felt, &c.	27	7	2
Wages of Attendants, &c.	498	19	8
POLICE—West Riding of Yorkshire Constabulary	8	7	1
POLICE—Durham County Constabulary	2	0	0
	£2,321	17	11

SUMMARY.

	£	s.	d.
Provisions, Fruit, Wines, Beer, Spirits, &c., &c.	1,311	12	7
Amusements	161	4	6
Fireworks	205	5	0
Accommodation, Tents, Lodgings, Police, Attendance, &c.	2,321	17	11
Grand Total	£4,000	0	0

TOAST LIST.

THE QUEEN ....By the CHAIRMAN.
Band .... "God save the Queen."

THE PRINCE AND PRINCESS OF WALES, AND THE REST
    OF THE ROYAL FAMILY .... By the CHAIRMAN.
Band..... ....…."God bless the Prince of Wales."

THE BISHOPS AND CLERGY.........By the EARL OF BRADFORD.
Band..................... ...."The Heavens are telling."
    Response by the Rev. JOHN SANDERSON.

THE ARMY, NAVY, AND RESERVE FORCES.
    By the CHAIRMAN.
Band......................................."British Grenadiers and Rule Britannia."
Responses by LORD MUNCASTER, M.P., and EDGAR A. DRUMMOND, ESQ.

VISCOUNT LUMLEY............By EDWARD DANNATT, ESQ.
Band... ...." Home Sweet Home."
    Response by VISCOUNT LUMLEY.

THE EARL AND COUNTESS OF SCARBROUGH.
    By WILLIAM EVERINGTON, ESQ.
Band.......................................…"The Fine Old English Gentleman."
    Response by the EARL OF SCARBROUGH.

THE HON. OSBERT LUMLEY, AND THE REST OF THE
    FAMILY...........................By JOHN CRAWFORD, ESQ.
Band.."Annie Laurie."
    Responses by the HON. OSBERT LUMLEY and EARL GROSVENOR.

THE TENANTS.................................." By the CHAIRMAN."
Band..."Auld Lang Syne."
    Response by W. J. NICHOLSON, ESQ.

SUCCESS TO TRADE AND AGRICULTURE.
    By VISCOUNT NEWPORT, M.P.
Band.." Speed the Plough."
    Responses by JOHN CLARK, ESQ., and GEO. WILLOWS, ESQ.

SUCCESS TO FOX HUNTING.........By the EARL OF ZETLAND.
Band. ...." We'll all go a-hunting to-day."   (Warwickshire Hunt.)
    Response by VISCOUNT GALWAY, M.P.

THE AGENT...........................By the CHAIRMAN.
Band.." The Oak and Ash."
    Response by H. V. TIPPET, ESQ.

THE LADIES.......................By BAILLIE COCHRANE, ESQ., M.P.
Band ...." Here's a health to all Good Lasses."
    Response by COUNT DONHOFF.

Index of recipes